The NEW ZEALAND LAMB *Cookbook*

NATURALLY TENDER NEW ZEALAND LAMB

Published by Martin Books
Simon & Schuster Consumer Group
Fitzwilliam House
32 Trumpington Street
Cambridge CB2 1QY

in association with
The New Zealand Meat Producers' Board
34-36 Grays Inn Road
London WC1X 8HR

First published 1991

ISBN 0 85941 707 7

Credits
Design: Ken Vail Graphic Design
Cover photograph: David Burch
Illustrations: Richard Jacobs
Printed and bound by Butler & Tanner Ltd,
Frome, Somerset

Recipe notes

Ingredients are listed in both metric and imperial measures. It is important to follow one set of quantities throughout, as they are not interchangeable.

Tablespoons (tbsp) and teaspoons (tsp) are standard British measuring spoons (15 ml and 5 ml respectively) and are assumed to be level.

Unless otherwise stated, herbs are assumed to be fresh.

Preparation and cooking timings are intended only as guides and are approximate.

Calorie counts are based on the assumption that the lamb is trimmed of excess fat.

Contents

Introduction

New Zealand's temperate climate, with rain and sunshine in perfect balance, is a wonderful environment for farming. Little surprise, then, that New Zealand Lamb is everything that lamb should be: naturally tasty, tender and delicious – just as the quality of the wine, honey, cheese, butter and fruit that New Zealand's farmers produce is widely accepted as second to none.

But it's not just New Zealand's natural environment that makes New Zealand lamb such a high-quality product: New Zealand's farms have extremely high standards, and great importance is given to the health and welfare of the animals. These high standards are maintained in the processing plants – some of the most modern and sophisticated in the world – where attention to hygiene and quality is meticulous.

New Zealand Lamb comes to Britain

Britain was New Zealand's first overseas customer when in 1882 New Zealand's first sailing ship with refrigeration facilities, the *Dunedin*, sailed into London after a hazardous journey lasting 98 days. Britain was suffering from a shortage of meat; New Zealand, with a small population and a surplus of lamb, required new markets. The result was a successful partnership that has grown to the point where more than 40 per cent of the lamb we consume comes from New Zealand.

All New Zealand Lamb is carefully selected and graded, and only the carcases that reach the required standard are sent for export. Quality control is stringent, and similar care is taken with the shipping conditions. Today's cargoes of frozen lamb travel in purpose-built container ships to ensure that the lamb arrives in tip-top condition, ready for immediate sale or cold storage.

High street butchers buy the lamb either as carcases or as ready-packed joints, while outlets like supermarkets and freezer centre chains have their meat butchered into convenient cuts to suit their own customers. These cuts are then vacuum packed to help maintain the appearance and quality of the lamb.

Each supermarket group or freezer centre chain has its own labelling system (names of cuts vary around the country, which is something to watch out for). You will now find cuts of New Zealand Lamb whose labels list not only the cut and its weight, but also detailed nutritional information, advice on thawing, cooking instructions and even recipes.

Buying New Zealand Lamb

New Zealand Lamb is widely available all year round, and is always in prime condition. Many consumers choose to buy their New Zealand Lamb from their local butcher, a man who can offer first-class advice. He's also the person to ask if you require something special, like a crown roast or guard of honour. Give him plenty of warning, though – a busy Saturday morning is not the time for sudden special requests!

Other shoppers may prefer the convenience of one-stop shopping, buying their lamb in the frozen packs described above. Supermarkets now carry joints, chops, leg steaks, neck fillet or stewing lamb, diced shoulder, mince and sliced liver.

The next few pages give you all the information you need about choosing, cooking and serving naturally tender New Zealand Lamb. You'll then find recipes for anything from a simple lamburger to an impressive loin of lamb with spinach stuffing. A range of roasts provides the perfect centrepiece for Sunday lunches, while weekday meals are made simple by a selection of family favourites that includes casseroles, grills, pies and bakes. There's fun on the menu when the children choose dishes like crunchy riblets or mini meatball pittas and whether you're dining in or eating outside, you'll find special occasion or barbecue recipes to fit the bill. Recipes from round the world are celebrated in Travellers' Tales, while the closing chapter is for the many microwave users who are discovering just how well tender New Zealand Lamb lends itself to this method of cooking.

Nutrition

Lamb is an important part of a healthy diet and contrary to the popular myth, it is not a fatty meat. Long before the current popular concerns about healthy eating, New Zealand had already introduced a policy of breeding leaner livestock. The result of this far-sighted attitude is an authentic, low-fat, low-cholesterol red meat, rich in protein and iron, which is available at a price most British households can afford.

New Zealand Lamb has a naturally low sodium content and a low ratio of sodium to potassium. A 100 g (4 oz) portion of cooked New Zealand Lamb, trimmed on the plate of most of the visible fat, would provide about 220 calories and about 13 g of fat – less than half of which would be saturated fat. An adult male would be provided with at least 30 per cent of his recommended daily amount (RDA) of protein, plus all the essential amino acids to help him utilise that protein effectively. The cholesterol content would compare favourably with that of beef, pork and even light chicken meat; and lean lamb contains considerably less cholesterol than dark chicken meat.

Lamb is a good source of B-group vitamins, particularly niacin and B12. In common with other meats, it is low in calcium and iodine but has significant amounts of iron and zinc, important for healthy growth in children, and for pregnant women.

A natural product, New Zealand Lamb is untainted by growth accelerators or other artificial substances. To take advantage of all its health-giving properties and to minimise the fat content, follow a few simple rules:

● Trim visible fat;

● Grill or dry-fry where possible;

● Pour off fat from fry-start casseroles;

● Skim soups, sauces, stocks and stews of surface fat, if necessary removing the fat in a solid layer after overnight chilling;

● Cook roasts on a rack wherever possible, to allow fat to drain;

● Skim off fat from pan juices before making gravies;

● Thicken sauces by natural reduction or by the addition of puréed vegetables, if possible.

The recipes in this cookbook have been prepared with sensible nutrition in view, with added fat kept to a minimum and consideration given to maximising the dietary fibre content of your meals. Grilling, rack-roasting, simmering and steaming are the healthiest ways to cook lamb; all are fully explored within these pages.

Finally, there are suggestions for suitable garnishes and accompaniments, including that other famous gift from New Zealand, the kiwi fruit, which is not only rich in vitamin C but which also has significant amounts of vitamin E.

Regional names for lamb cuts

Lamb cuts are often known by different names in different parts of the country. Here are some of the alternatives:

Whole leg	'gigot'
Half leg fillet	'fillet', 'shank';
Half leg knuckle	'shank';
Chump chops	'leg chops', 'gigot chops';
Best end of neck	'cutlets', 'fine end', 'single loin';
Breast	'lap', 'flank'.
Double loin (cut across the whole carcase)	'Barnsley', 'butterfly'
Double loin	'cut double thickness'
Leg bone steaks	'gigot chops'

Choosing the correct cut

New Zealand Lamb is available in a wide range of cuts, either direct from the high street butcher or neatly packaged and labelled in supermarket or freezer centre cabinets. On the following pages you will find full colour pictures of the most common cuts, plus tables listing how best – and for how long – to cook them.

Lamb should be thoroughly thawed before cooking; see pages 10–11 for advice on the best ways of thawing different cuts. Use moderate heat when cooking New Zealand Lamb. Unless recipes state otherwise, roast at 180°C/350°F/Gas Mark 4.

Check the cooking time chart opposite and read the box on 'How to cook a perfect roast joint' on page 11, for the best results when roasting New Zealand Lamb.

Adjust the timings to suit your personal preference; if you like your lamb pink, choose the minimum time, if you prefer it well done, opt for the upper limit.

Neck ring

Shoulder

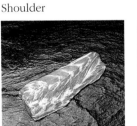

Neck fillet

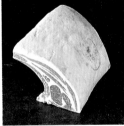

Best end

Minced lamb

Loin chops

Chump chops

Leg

Cooking time chart		
Cut	Cooking method	Time
Leg, whole or half per 450 g (1 lb)	roast	25–30 minutes
Shoulder, whole or half per 450 g (1 lb)	roast	25–30 minutes
Shoulder, boned, rolled and stuffed per 450 g (1 lb)	roast	40–45 minutes
Best end of neck	roast	1¼–1¾ hours (total)
Best end cutlets	grill	15–18 minutes
Breast per 450 g (1 lb)	roast	30–45 minutes
Breast, boned, rolled and stuffed per 450 g (1 lb)	roast	40–45 minutes
Loin chops (2.5 cm/1-inch)	grill	18–22 minutes (total)
Loin chops (4 cm/1½-inch)	grill	20–24 minutes (total)
Loin chops (5 cm/2-inch)	grill	22–26 minutes (total)
Chump chops per 450 g (1 lb)	grill braise	20–25 minutes (total) 45 minutes
Loin	roast	1¼–2¼ hours (total)
Stewing lamb per 450 g (1 lb)	braise	1 hour
Diced lamb stew/casserole kebabs	braise grill	1½–2 hours (total) 20–25 minutes (total)
Minced lamb 100 g (4 oz) burgers	grill	12 minutes (total)
Liver, thinly sliced casserole	fry bake	15–20 minutes (total) 1–1½ hours (total)

Thawing and freezing

New Zealand Lamb can be safely stored in your freezer for up to 6 months. To preserve the flavour and succulent quality of lamb, always thaw it carefully and thoroughly before cooking. Cooking lamb from frozen is *not* recommended as this results in greater shrinkage, is difficult to time correctly and can result in flavour loss.

Most supermarkets sell frozen New Zealand Lamb in a very strong vacuum pack. You can thaw it either in or out of the wrapping. Thawing in the wrap is more convenient but takes longer. For quicker thawing, simply remove the wrap and put the meat on a plate, loosely covered. Whichever method you choose, if time permits slow thawing in the fridge will bring out the best flavour of the meat. Once it is thawed, it is preferable to allow the meat to come to room temperature before cooking.

Refrigerator thawing

Smaller cuts such as chops, steaks or noisettes will take 5–7 hours in the fridge, depending on their size. For joints weighing less than 1.4 kg (3½ lb), allow 3–4 hours per 450 g (1 lb). Larger joints will require 4–7 hours per 450 g (1 lb). An average leg of New Zealand Lamb will take about 24 hours to thaw.

Microwave thawing (700 watt appliance)

Lamb chops: Arrange the chops around the rim of a plate with the thin ends pointing towards the centre. Set the microwave to Defrost and allow 5 minutes per 450 g (1 lb). Turn the chops over half-way through thawing.

Minced lamb: Place in a dish. Allow 5 minutes per 450 g (1 lb) on Defrost. Break up the mince with a fork as it defrosts.

Diced lamb: Place in a dish. Allow 5 minutes per 450 g (1 lb) on Defrost. Move the pieces around half-way through thawing.

Joints: Place on a plate. Allow 10 minutes per 450 g (1 lb) on Defrost, turning the meat over half-way through thawing. Check for 'hot spots', and shield them by covering them with small pieces of foil. At the end of the thawing time, let the meat stand for at least 10 minutes to equalise the temperature.

Note: For microwaves with a lower power output than 700 watts it may be necessary to adjust the thawing times.

Freezing cooked lamb dishes

Freeze casseroles and bakes before garnishing but after removing any excess fat from the surface. Use freezerproof dishes, cartons or foil containers. Overwrap if necessary, seal and label. Store sauces in polyboxes separately from the meat. Use within 3 months.

How to cook a perfect roast joint

1. Weigh the joint, including any stuffing, and calculate the cooking time from the chart on page 9.

2. Place the joint in a shallow tin, preferably on a grid so it doesn't sit in the fat and meat juices that run off the meat during cooking.

3. If the joint is quite lean, baste it with a little melted fat.

4. Roast the lamb for the calculated cooking time in a preheated oven at 180°C/350°F/Gas Mark 4.

5. To enhance the lamb's delicate flavour, try sprinkling it with fresh herbs such as marjoram mixed with grated lemon rind and juice. Or insert slivers of garlic and rosemary leaves into small cuts in the joint's surface.

Carving

Having cooked the perfect joint, it would be a shame to hack it to bits! Careful carving not only looks good, it also makes the meat go further, so it is a skill well worth acquiring.

Roast lamb will be easier to carve if you cover it loosely with a tent of foil and allow it to rest for 10–15 minutes after it comes out of the oven. *Equipment:* A spiked carving dish, though not essential, is a great help in holding the meat steady, especially if you are inexperienced.

Always use a carving fork with a thumb guard, and choose your knife with care. A knife with a 25 cm (10-inch) blade is ideal. Sharpen it before use, using a traditional steel or an electric knife sharpener. Alternatively, use an electric carving knife. This easy-to-use appliance makes carving thin slices simplicity itself. Treat it with care and always remove the blades and unplug the knife as soon as you have finished using it. Any knife is dangerous in the wrong hands, but a small child who switches on an electric carving knife could

Carving a shoulder of lamb
1 Before cooking, insert a sharp pointed knife and cut all round to loosen blade bone.
2 Cooking will shrink meat, exposing end of blade bone. Twist right round completely and pull it out.
3 Cut thin slices of meat using a sharp carving knife, working from outside in.
4 When bone is reached, turn joint over and continue carving. Repeat until all meat is removed.

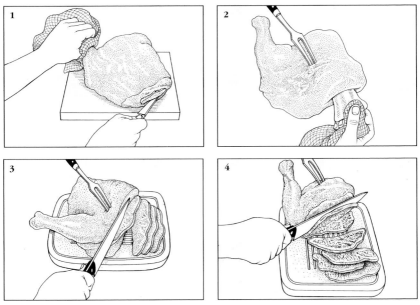

be seriously injured.

Boned joints: The easiest joints to carve are those which have been boned and rolled. Remove some of the skewers and strings, but leave sufficient of these in place to maintain the shape of the joint. Aim to carve neat slices of consistent width, removing the remaining skewers or strings as you come upon them. Use a long, even, sawing action, keeping the blade of the knife at the same angle all the time. Do not press down on the meat too much or you will squeeze out some of the juices.

Bone-in joints: Having a bone to contend with makes carving more difficult, but don't panic. Carving is an accomplishment like any other, and can easily be mastered. There are no absolute rules. The step-by-step illustrations on these pages show how easy it can be to reduce a leg of lamb or shoulder to neat, manageable slices. Try to cut the lamb against the grain wherever possible, as this will give more tender slices. When carving becomes difficult, turn the joint over and begin again.

Have heated serving plates ready – and if possible

Carving a leg of lamb
1 Use a cloth to hold the shank end of the joint and turn the meatiest side of the joint uppermost. Take out two slices, about 1/4 in. thick, from the centre of the leg, cutting to the bone.
2 Continue slicing from both sides of the first cut, and gradually angling the knife to obtain longer slices.
3 For the underside, turn the joint over, remove any unwanted fat and carve in long horizontal slices.

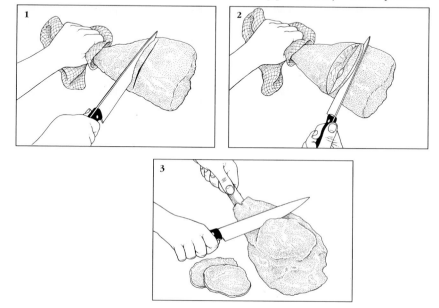

persuade someone else to dish up the vegetables. Being carver and server is a juggling act no one should be called upon to perform by themselves.

Lastly, don't worry if your first efforts are less than perfect: at least you can eat the evidence!

Herbs, marinades and sauces

Herbs, spices and fruit

Lamb has an affinity with a wide variety of flavours. Mint sauce is the time-honoured British accompaniment, but try tucking slivers of garlic and rosemary leaves into slits in a leg or shoulder of lamb before roasting it on a bed of root vegetables: you will find it a combination difficult to better – until you sample the southern Mediterranean mixture of lamb, aubergines, tomatoes and oregano in a dish like Lamb Ratatouille Pie.

Sharp fruits contrast perfectly with the sweetness of New Zealand lamb. Redcurrants, oranges, lemons and kiwi fruit all feature in the recipes that follow, while dried fruits such as apricots and prunes find favour in casseroles and stuffings.

Taking the spice route to produce rich lamb curries is equally successful, and even the simplest of dishes can be enhanced by a little parsley or dill.

Sage is favoured by the Italians, with good reason. It gives a warm, strong flavour to stuffings, minced lamb and liver dishes. Tarragon, used sparingly, is very good in casseroles and on grills.

Herbs and spices should always be used judiciously. New Zealand Lamb is the most delectable of meats: its flavour should be enhanced but never overwhelmed by its accompaniments.

Marinades

Use marinades to add a special flavour to lamb. Marinades also help to keep the lamb moist and succulent, and so are very effective when the lamb is cooked on a high heat, as on a barbecue.

Typical marinade ingredients include oil, fruit juice, wine, herbs and spices. The acids – for example from wine or fruit juice – act as tenderisers, while flooding the meat with flavour.

It is important to marinate the meat in a china, glass or stainless steel dish, to ensure there is no acid reaction which could taint the flavour. Make sure the dish is large enough to hold the joint to be marinated: in the case of pieces of lamb, the dish should be able to hold the meat in a single layer.

Allow about 125 ml (4 fl oz) of marinade for every 450 g (1 lb) of meat. Cubes are usually marinated for a relatively short time (2–3 hours) while whole joints may be marinated overnight. Longer is not necessarily better; excessively long marination may make the meat too pungent and spoil its natural flavour.

If meat is to be marinated for over 1 hour, cover it closely to avoid transference of flavours and place it in the refrigerator.

Sauces

A sauce may be as simple as fresh cream stirred into the skimmed cooking juices, or be more elaborate than the main attraction.

The intrinsic flavour of the lamb should be heightened by the sauce that accompanies it. Avoid heavy, over-seasoned sauces and concentrate instead on mixtures that will enhance not merely the taste but also the appearance of the finished dish. A delicate orange and ginger sauce, for instance, is the perfect accompaniment, both visually and in terms of flavour, to lamb leg steaks. For lamb with walnut and basil stuffing, a more robust sauce, using tomatoes, herbs and Worcestershire sauce, is needed.

Ingredients are very important. Stock should always be of good quality, preferably home-made. Use fresh herbs wherever possible (halve the quantity if using dried) and don't skimp on the stirring.

A selection of simple, practical dishes for mid-week meals. The recipes range from slow-cooked casseroles that will take care of themselves – ideal for those hectic days when you seem to be running a taxi service for the entire neighbourhood – to grills, gougères and bakes which can be swiftly prepared at the end of a working day.

Sweet and Sour Lamb

Serves: *4*

Preparation time: *about 15 minutes*

Cooking time: *25 minutes*

Calories per portion: *490*

*4 large **New Zealand Lamb** loin chops, trimmed*

Sauce:
1 tbsp oil
1 onion, chopped
1 garlic clove, crushed
1 large eating apple, quartered, cored and sliced
50 g (2 oz) raisins
4 tbsp red wine vinegar
3 tbsp orange juice
4 tbsp soft light brown sugar
2 tbsp water
salt and pepper

1. First make the sauce. Heat the oil in a saucepan and fry the onion and garlic until soft and lightly coloured. Add the remaining ingredients and bring to the boil, stirring. Lower the heat and simmer, stirring occasionally, for about 10 minutes until the sauce is reduced by about one third. Adjust the seasoning and keep warm.
2. Arrange the chops on a foil-lined grill rack. Cook under moderate heat for 5–8 minutes on each side until well browned and cooked through.
3. Transfer the chops to a heated serving dish, pour the sauce over and serve.

Coromandel Lamb Goulash

Serves: *8*

Preparation time:
15 minutes

Cooking time:
3 hours

Calories per portion: *315*

900 g (2 lb) **New Zealand Lamb** *shoulder, trimmed and diced*
25 g (1 oz) butter
1 onion, sliced
2 carrots, sliced
2 tbsp paprika
3 tbsp plain flour
1.2 litres (2 pints) warm lamb stock
salt and pepper
150 ml (¼ pint) natural yogurt
Minty dumplings:
100 g (4 oz) self-raising flour
50 g (2 oz) suet
1 tbsp dried mint
about 6 tbsp cold water

1. Set the oven at 150°/300°F/Gas Mark 2. Melt the butter in a large frying-pan. Add the diced lamb and fry until evenly browned. Remove the meat from the pan with a slotted spoon and place in an ovenproof dish.

Coromandel Lamb Goulash

2. Add the onion and carrots to the fat remaining in the pan and fry for about 5 minutes or until soft. With the slotted spoon, add the vegetables to the meat.
3. Sprinkle the paprika and flour into the pan and fry for 2 minutes, stirring constantly. Gradually add the stock, with salt and pepper to taste. Bring to the boil and pour over the lamb and vegetables. Cover the ovenproof dish with a lid or foil and bake for 2½–3 hours or until the meat is tender.
4. Make the dumplings. Mix the flour, suet and mint in a bowl, adding salt and pepper to taste. Stir in enough water to make a soft but not sticky dough. Divide into 8 small dumplings and add these to the goulash 30 minutes before the end of the cooking time.
5. Stir in the yogurt just before serving, or pour it into a jug and offer it separately.

Lamb and Cranberry Puffs

Serves: *4*

Preparation time: *20 minutes*

Cooking time: *35–40 minutes*

Calories per portion: *485*

4 *New Zealand Lamb* best end cutlets, trimmed
4 tbsp cranberry sauce
225 g (8 oz) packet of frozen puff pastry, thawed
flour for rolling
beaten egg to glaze
Garnish:
watercress
orange slices

1. Set the oven at 200°C/400°F/Gas Mark 6. Place 1 tbsp cranberry sauce on each cutlet.
2. Roll out the pastry on a floured board to a rectangle measuring 30 × 20 cm (12 × 8 inches). Brush with egg and cut into 8 strips, each 2.5 cm (1 inch) wide.
3. Wrap 2 pastry strips around each sauce-topped cutlet, starting at the base and overlapping the edges a little. Press to seal.
4. Place the pastry-wrapped cutlets on a baking sheet and brush with egg. Bake for 35–40 minutes until the pastry is golden-brown. Serve garnished with watercress and orange slices.

Campbell Lamb and Bean Layer

Serves: *4*

Preparation time:
5–10 minutes

Cooking time:
45 minutes

Calories per portion: *485*

575 g (1¼ lb) **New Zealand Lamb** *shoulder or fillet, trimmed and diced*
1 onion, sliced thinly
2 garlic cloves, crushed
1 tbsp tomato purée
150 ml (¼ pint) lamb or vegetable stock
100 g (4 oz) mushrooms, sliced or quartered
salt and pepper
1 tsp dried mixed herbs
1 tsp Worcestershire sauce
425 g (15 oz) can of flageolet beans
425 g (15 oz) can of red kidney beans
40 g (1½ oz) Cheddar cheese, grated
White sauce:
25 g (1 oz) butter or margarine
25 g (1 oz) plain flour
300 ml (½ pint) milk

1. Put the lamb into a heavy-bottomed saucepan with the onion and garlic. Heat gently until the fat starts to run. Raise the heat and cook until the lamb is well sealed, stirring from time to time.
2. Add the tomato purée, stock, mushrooms, salt and pepper, herbs and Worcestershire sauce. Bring to the boil, lower the heat, cover and simmer for 20 minutes.
3. Meanwhile tip the contents of both cans of beans into a saucepan and heat gently.
4. Make the white sauce. Melt the fat in a saucepan, stir in the flour and cook for 1 minute. Gradually stir in the milk and bring to the boil, stirring constantly. Lower the heat and simmer for 2 minutes, then add plenty of salt and pepper to taste.
5. Drain the beans thoroughly and put half in the base of a large casserole. Spoon the lamb mixture over them and cover with the rest of the beans. Top with the white sauce and sprinkle with the cheese.
6. Brown the cheese topping under a moderate grill. Serve with crusty bread and a green salad.

Beanie Lamb Hotpot

Serves: *4*

Preparation time:
10 minutes + soaking

Cooking time:
2½ hours

Calories per portion: *750*

Beanie Lamb Hotpot

675 g (1½ lb) **New Zealand Lamb** *stewing lamb, trimmed*
75 g (3 oz) dried red kidney beans
75 g (3 oz) dried black-eyed beans
75 g (3 oz) dried mung beans
1 tbsp oil
2 onions, sliced
4 carrots, sliced
4 celery sticks, sliced
600 ml (1 pint) lamb or chicken stock
salt and pepper
1 bay leaf
chopped parsley to garnish

1. Put the red kidney beans in a bowl with cold water to cover. In a second bowl, combine the black-eyed beans and mung beans. Add water to cover. Soak the beans overnight.

2. Next day, drain the kidney beans, rinse under fresh water and place in a saucepan. Add fresh water to cover, bring to the boil and boil vigorously for 20 minutes. Drain, then place in a large casserole with the drained black-eyed and mung beans.

3. Set the oven at 160°C/325°F/Gas Mark 3. Heat the oil in a large frying-pan, add the vegetables and cook for 2–3 minutes. Using a slotted spoon, transfer the vegetables to the casserole.

4. Add the lamb to the fat remaining in the frying-pan and fry until golden-brown, turning once. Add the stock, salt, pepper and bay leaf. Bring the stock to the boil, stirring to incorporate any sediment on the base of the pan, then add to the casserole.

5. Cover the casserole and bake for 2 hours or until the meat and the beans are tender. Remove the bay leaf.

6. Sprinkle the hotpot with the chopped parsley and serve at once, with crusty french bread, if liked.

Lamb-Stuffed Peppers

Serves: *4*	*350 g (12 oz) minced* **New Zealand Lamb**
Preparation time: *10 minutes*	*100 g (4 oz) brown rice*
	1 onion, chopped
Cooking time: *1–1¼ hours*	*397 g (14 oz) can of chopped tomatoes*
	2 tsp salt
Calories per portion: *350*	*freshly ground black pepper*
	½ tsp ground cinnamon
	25 g (1 oz) walnut pieces
	4 large green, red or yellow peppers

1. Cook the rice in a saucepan of boiling salted water for 35–40 minutes. Drain thoroughly.

2. Meanwhile set the oven at 180°C/350°F/Gas Mark 4. Combine the lamb and onion in a large heavy-bottomed saucepan. Heat gently until the fat runs, then raise the heat and fry until the lamb is browned. Add the tomatoes with their juices. Stir in 2 tsp salt, a generous grinding of pepper and the cinnamon. Lower the heat, cover the pan and simmer for 20 minutes. Stir in the walnut pieces.

3. Cut a lid, 1 cm (½ inch) deep, from the stalk end of each pepper. Scoop out the core and seeds. Place the peppers and lids in a saucepan with boiling salted water to cover. Cook for 2 minutes. Using a slotted spoon, remove the peppers from the water and place upside down on absorbent kitchen paper to drain.

4. Mix the rice with the meat mixture and fill the peppers. Replace the lids. Stand the filled peppers in a shallow ovenproof dish, spooning any remaining filling around them.

5. Bake for 30 minutes, then serve at once

Queenstown Casserole

Serves: *4*

Preparation time: *about 25 minutes*

Cooking time: *1½ – 1¾ hours*

Calories per portion: *930*

900 g (2 lb) **New Zealand Lamb**, *stewing lamb, trimmed*
25 g (1 oz) butter or margarine
2 tbsp plain flour
3 tbsp tomato purée
salt and pepper
600 ml (1 pint) lamb or vegetable stock or water
½ tsp dried oregano or marjoram
1 tbsp oil
3 onions, sliced
4 carrots, sliced
2 turnips, diced
8 small potatoes

1. Lay the lamb rings in a grill pan. Cook under moderate heat, turning once, until lightly browned.

2. Melt the fat in a large flameproof casserole or saucepan. Stir in the flour and tomato purée and cook for 1 minute. Gradually add the stock and bring to the boil. Season well and add the herbs. Add the lamb to the casserole, lower the heat, cover and

simmer very gently for 1 hour, stirring occasionally.
3. Meanwhile heat the oil in a frying-pan. Add the onion and fry until soft but not coloured. Using a slotted spoon, transfer the onion to the casserole, with the carrots and turnips. Cover the casserole again and simmer for 15 minutes more.
4. Peel but do not slice the potatoes. Add them to the casserole and simmer for a further 20 minutes or until the potatoes are just tender.
5. Adjust the seasoning, skim off any fat from the surface of the casserole and serve.

Lamb Ratatouille Pie

Serves: *6*

Preparation time: *35 minutes*

Cooking time: *55–60 minutes*

Calories per portion: *470*

*½ leg of **New Zealand Lamb** (fillet end), about 800 g (1¾ lb), trimmed and cubed*
2 tbsp plain flour
salt and pepper
1 tbsp oil
1 garlic clove, crushed
1 large onion, chopped
397 g (14 oz) can of chopped tomatoes
1 tbsp tomato purée
1 tsp dried oregano
1 red pepper, cored, de-seeded and chopped
1 aubergine, sliced
225 g (8 oz) courgettes, sliced thinly
Pastry:
175 g (6 oz) plain flour, plus extra for rolling
75 g (3 oz) butter or margarine
50 g (2 oz) Cheddar cheese, grated
1 tsp mustard powder
1–2 tbsp cold water
beaten egg or milk to glaze

1. Mix the flour, salt and pepper in a paper or polythene bag, add the lamb cubes and toss until evenly coated.
2. Heat the oil in a saucepan, add the garlic and onion and fry for about 5 minutes until soft. Add the lamb and fry until evenly coloured. Add the tomatoes,

tomato purée and oregano, then bring to the boil.
3. Lower the heat, cover and simmer for 25 minutes, then stir in the chopped pepper. Set aside to cool.
4. Set the oven at 200°C/400°F/Gas Mark 6. Cook the aubergine slices in boiling salted water for 3 minutes, then drain and dry on absorbent kitchen paper.
5. To make the pastry, place the flour in a bowl. Rub in the fat until the mixture resembles fine breadcrumbs. Stir in the cheese and mustard. Add enough water to make a firm dough. Knead lightly.
6. Place half the lamb mixture in the base of a 1.2-litre (2-pint) pie dish. Cover with the aubergine slices, then the courgettes. Place the remaining lamb on top.
7. Roll out the pastry on a floured board. Cover the pie. Brush with egg or milk and bake for 35–40 minutes until the pastry is crisp and golden-brown. Serve hot or cold.

Lamb Ratatouille Pie

Lamb and Kidney Kebabs

Serves: *4*

Preparation time:
25 minutes + marinating

Cooking time:
7–10 minutes

Calories per portion: *280*

450 g (1 lb) lean **New Zealand Lamb** *shoulder or leg, trimmed and diced*

4 New Zealand Lamb's kidneys, trimmed and cut in half

1 green pepper, cored, de-seeded and blanched in boiling water

100 g (4 oz) button mushrooms

8 tomatoes, quartered

8 bay leaves

salt and pepper

Marinade:

2 tbsp oil

1 tbsp vinegar

1 garlic clove, crushed

1 onion, chopped roughly

salt and pepper

Lamb and Kidney Kebabs

1. Combine all the ingredients for the marinade in a large bowl. Add the lamb cubes and kidneys, turning until thoroughly coated. Cover and marinate overnight.

2. Drain the lamb, reserving the marinade. Cut the green pepper into bite-sized pieces. Wipe the mushrooms.

3. Thread the lamb and vegetables alternately on to 4 large skewers, beginning and ending with a bay leaf. Season with salt and pepper.

4. Cook the kebabs on a barbecue or under the grill for 7–10 minutes, turning once and basting with the reserved marinade.

Lamb'n'Leeks

Serves: *3*

Preparation time: *20 minutes*

Cooking time: *about 1 hour 20 minutes*

Calories per portion: 565

*½ shoulder of **New Zealand Lamb** (knuckle end), about 800 g (1¾ lb), trimmed*

salt and pepper

1 tbsp oil

6–8 whole cloves

450 g (1 lb) leeks, trimmed

225 g (8 oz) carrots

150 ml (¼ pint) lamb or vegetable stock

2 tbsp wine vinegar

Sauce:

25 g (1 oz) margarine

25 g (1 oz) plain flour

300 ml (½ pint) cooking juices (see method)

3 tbsp single cream

a pinch of ground coriander

1. Set the oven at 200°C/400°/Gas Mark 6. Wipe the lamb and sprinkle lightly with salt and pepper. Stand it in a small roasting tin or fairly shallow casserole. Brush the oil over the joint and stud the top with cloves. Roast for 20 minutes.

2. Meanwhile cut the leeks into 2.5 cm (1-inch) lengths and the carrots into thick strips about 5 cm (2 inches) long. Place in a saucepan of water and bring to the boil. Drain.

3. Pour off any fat from around the lamb. Arrange the blanched vegetables around the meat. Add the stock and vinegar, cover with foil or a lid and return to the oven for $3/4$–1 hour or until the lamb is tender. Remove the foil or lid for the last 10 minutes to brown the skin.

4. Strain off the cooking juices into a measuring jug. Skim off any fat from the surface and make the cooking juices up to 300 ml ($1/2$ pint) with water if necessary. Transfer the lamb to a heated serving dish and surround with the vegetables. Keep warm.

5. Make the sauce. Melt the margarine in a saucepan, stir in the flour and cook for 1 minute. Gradually add the cooking juices and bring to the boil. Lower the heat, stir in the cream and simmer for 2 minutes. Adjust the seasoning, adding the coriander, then strain into a sauce boat.

6. Serve the lamb and vegetables, offering the sauce separately. Jacket potatoes, baked alongside the lamb, make a simple but very good accompaniment.

Liver with Orange

Serves: *4*

Preparation time: *5 minutes*

Cooking time: *12 minutes*

Calories per portion: *365*

450 g (1 lb) **New Zealand Lamb** 's liver, trimmed and sliced thinly
65 g (2½ oz) butter
1 onion, chopped finely
5 tbsp freshly-squeezed orange juice
1 orange, peeled and cut into segments
1 tbsp chopped parsley

1. Melt half the butter in a frying-pan, add the onion and fry for about 5 minutes or until golden.

2. Raise the heat, add the liver and fry quickly, turning frequently, for 2–3 minutes on each side, until golden outside but still pink in the centre. Using a slotted spoon, transfer the liver to a heated serving dish and keep hot.

3. Add the orange juice and orange segments to the fat remaining in the pan. Heat through, stirring constantly.

4. Remove the orange segments with a slotted spoon and arrange them around the liver.
5. Remove the pan from the heat and stir in the parsley, with the remaining butter. Pour the sauce over the lamb and orange segments. Serve at once.

Lamb Chops Gougère

Serves: *4*

Preparation time:
10 minutes

Cooking time:
35–40 minutes

Calories per portion: *475*

4 ***New Zealand Lamb*** *loin chops, trimmed*
1 garlic clove, cut in half
1 tsp oil
1 onion, sliced
1 tsp dried mixed herbs
2 tomatoes, quartered, to garnish
Choux pastry:
50 g (2 oz) margarine
150 ml (¼ pint) water
75 g (3 oz) plain flour
2 large eggs, beaten
½ tsp salt and pepper to taste
1 tsp French mustard

1. Set the oven at 200°C/400°F/Gas Mark 6. Rub the chops all over with the cut clove of garlic. Use a little of the oil to grease a shallow ovenproof dish or roasting tin. Arrange the onion slices over the base of the tin and sprinkle with the herbs. Drizzle the remaining oil over the top and cover with the chops.
2. Make the choux pastry. Combine the margarine and water in a small saucepan. Heat gently until the margarine melts, then bring to the boil. Add the flour all at once. Immediately remove the saucepan from the heat and beat the mixture until it is smooth and thick and leaves the sides of the pan clean. Cool slightly, then beat in the eggs, a little at a time, with the salt. Add pepper to taste and stir in the mustard. Place spoonfuls of the mixture around the edge of the dish containing the chops.
3. Place the dish on a baking sheet and bake for 35–40 minutes until the pastry is crisp and brown. Garnish with the tomatoes and serve at once.

Sunday Best

The traditional roast remains one of the most popular ways of serving lamb: eight out of ten households have a roast meal of some sort at least once a week. It may be the only meal at which every member of the family sits down at the same time, so make it memorable. Here are some wonderful new ways of serving this all-time favourite.

Lamb with Nut and Crumb Topping

Serves: *3*

Preparation time: *20 minutes*

Cooking time: *about 1¼ hours*

Calories per portion: *315*

*½ shoulder of **New Zealand Lamb** (knuckle end), about 800 g (1¾ lb)*
salt and pepper
1 tbsp margarine, softened
parsley to garnish
Topping:
40 g (1½ oz) soft brown or white breadcrumbs
1½ tsp dried mixed herbs
25 g (1 oz) walnuts or pecan nuts, chopped
1 tbsp grated lemon zest
salt and pepper

1. Set the oven at 200°C/400°F/Gas Mark 6. Place the lamb in a small roasting tin or shallow casserole. Sprinkle lightly with salt and pepper and spread with softened margarine.
2. Prepare the topping by mixing the breadcrumbs, herbs, chopped nuts, lemon zest, salt and pepper in a bowl.
3. Roast the lamb for 45 minutes, then remove from the oven. Baste well, then spoon the breadcrumb mixture evenly over the surface, pressing it down with the back of the spoon. Return the lamb to the oven and bake for 25 minutes more or until cooked through.
4. Transfer the lamb to a heated serving dish, garnish with parsley and serve at once. If liked, the joint may be surrounded with duchesse potatoes and brussels sprouts.

Roast Lamb with Almonds

Serves: *8*

Preparation time:
15 minutes + marinating

Cooking time:
1½ – 2 hours

Calories per portion: *625*

*1 leg of **New Zealand Lamb**, about 2 kg (4½ lb), trimmed*

50 g (2 oz) blanched almonds

Marinade:
grated zest and juice of 1 lemon
4 tbsp oil
1 garlic clove, crushed
2 tbsp chopped parsley
salt and pepper

Sauce:
300 ml (½ pint) mayonnaise
grated zest and juice of 1 lemon
2 garlic cloves, crushed
50 g (2 oz) ground almonds
3 tbsp chopped parsley
strips of lemon zest

1. Put the lamb into a shallow dish. Mix all the marinade ingredients in a bowl and pour over the lamb. Cover the dish with cling film and leave in a cool place overnight, turning the joint over once.

2. Next day, set the oven at 180°C/350°F/Gas Mark 4. Remove the lamb from the dish, reserving the marinade. With a sharp knife, make small slits all over the lamb and insert the almonds.

3. Put the lamb in a roasting tin, pour over the reserved marinade and roast for 1½–2 hours or until cooked. Baste the joint several times during cooking. If the almonds start to become too brown, cover the joint with foil.

4. Meanwhile make the sauce. In a bowl, mix the mayonnaise with the lemon zest and juice, garlic and ground almonds. Add 2 tbsp of the parsley, with salt and pepper to taste. Mix well, then spoon into a small serving bowl. Sprinkle the remaining parsley over the top and add a couple of strips of lemon zest for effect.

5. Transfer the lamb to a heated serving dish and serve at once, accompanied by the sauce.

Loin of Lamb with Spinach Stuffing

Serves: 6

Preparation time:
45 minutes

Cooking time:
1½ hours

Calories per portion: 960

*1 boned and rolled double loin of **New Zealand
Lamb**, 1.4–1.6 kg (3–3½ lb), trimmed*
salt and pepper

Stuffing:
225 g (8 oz) frozen leaf spinach, thawed
75 g (3 oz) long-grain rice, cooked
1 carrot, grated coarsely
40 g (1½ oz) cashew nuts, chopped roughly
¼ tsp ground coriander
1 egg, beaten
2 tbsp oil

Gravy:
3 dsp plain flour
150 ml (¼ pint) white wine
300 ml (½ pint) lamb or vegetable stock
1 tsp tomato purée
2 tsp soy sauce
40 g (1½ oz) cashew nuts, chopped

Garnish:
12 even-sized roasting potatoes
cooked carrot sticks
parsley sprigs

1. Set the oven at 200°C/400°F/Gas Mark 6. On a board, open out the lamb and season the inside lightly with salt and pepper.

2. Make the stuffing. Drain the spinach, mashing it against the sides of the colander to remove the excess water. Chop the spinach roughly and put it in a bowl, with the rice, carrot, nuts and coriander. Season with salt and pepper and bind with the egg.

3. Spread the stuffing evenly over the inside of the lamb, carefully roll up again and secure with skewers and string. Weigh the stuffed lamb and calculate the cooking time at 30 minutes per 450 g (1 lb). Stand the lamb in a roasting tin. Brush all over with the oil, season lightly with salt and pepper and roast for 30 minutes.

4. Meanwhile peel the potatoes, keeping an even

Make the most of your butcher!

Your butcher can be your best friend when it comes to making the most of New Zealand Lamb. He'll gladly introduce you to any cuts that may be unfamiliar. Given a few days' notice he will also be happy to bone out a shoulder or leg joint for you, or to prepare a crown roast, double loin of lamb or a guard of honour if you want something special for a dinner party.

shape. Cut a strip off the base of each so that they stand evenly, then make deep cuts almost through to the base at 5 mm (¼-inch) intervals.

5. Remove the roasting tin from the oven, arrange the potatoes around the lamb and baste with fat. Continue to roast for the remainder of the calculated cooking time (about 1 hour) or until the lamb is cooked and the potatoes have fanned out and turned golden.

6. Remove the lamb to a heated serving platter and arrange the cooked carrot sticks around it. Transfer the potatoes to a heated serving dish. Keep warm.

7. Make the gravy. Pour off all but 1 tbsp of the juices from the roasting tin. Stir in the flour and cook for 1 minute. Gradually add the wine, stock, tomato purée and soy sauce. Bring to the boil, stirring constantly. Lower the heat and simmer for 2–3 minutes, then strain into a sauce boat. Stir in the chopped nuts.

8. Garnish the lamb with parsley and serve with the fantail potatoes and cashew nut gravy.

Loin of Lamb with
Spinach Stuffing

Wairoa Lamb Pot Roast

Serves: 5

Preparation time: *about 20 minutes, plus soaking*

Cooking time: *3–3½ hours*

Calories per portion: *930*

1 small leg of **New Zealand Lamb**, *about 1.8 kg (4 lb), trimmed*

225 g (8 oz) mixed dried beans, soaked overnight

2–3 garlic cloves, cut into thin slivers

a few sprigs of fresh rosemary

1 tbsp oil

1 large onion, chopped

3 celery sticks, sliced

4 carrots, cut into thick sticks

450 ml (¾ pint) lamb or vegetable stock

4 tbsp white wine

salt and pepper

a few sprigs of rosemary to garnish

1. Drain the beans, rinse under fresh water and place in a saucepan. Add fresh water to cover, bring to the boil and boil vigorously for 10

Wairoa Lamb Pot-Roast

minutes. Lower the heat, cover the pan and simmer for 30–40 minutes more. Drain the beans and set them aside.

2. Set the oven at 220°C/425°F/Gas Mark 7. Using a sharp knife, make cuts in the lamb, pressing a garlic sliver and a rosemary leaf into each.

3. Heat the oil in a saucepan, add the onion and fry until soft. Add the celery, carrots, stock and wine, with salt and pepper to taste. Bring to the boil, add the reserved beans and mix well.

4. Turn the bean mixture into a large ovenproof casserole. Stand the lamb on top, pressing the joint evenly into the beans. Cover tightly with foil and cook for 2½ hours, removing the foil for the last 30 minutes of the cooking time. The lamb should be cooked through and well browned.

5. Transfer the lamb to a wooden board. Drain the bean and vegetable mixture, reserving the pan juices in a jug. Spread the beans and vegetables on a heated serving dish, top with the lamb and garnish with rosemary. Skim off the fat from the pan juices and serve the juices with the lamb, if liked.

Lamb Orangery

Serves: *3*

Preparation time: *25 minutes*

Cooking time: *1½ hours*

Calories per portion: *345*

*½ leg of **New Zealand Lamb** (fillet end) boned and rolled, about 800 g (1¾ lb), trimmed*

125 ml (4 fl oz) orange juice
salt and pepper
thinly pared zest of 1 orange, cut into narrow strips
2 tsp cornflour
1 tbsp water
150 ml (¼ pint) lamb or vegetable stock
1 tbsp brandy
2 tsp redcurrant jelly
Garnish:
toasted flaked almonds
parsley sprigs

1. Set the oven at 190°C/375°F/Gas Mark 5. Place

the lamb in a casserole or small roasting tin. Pour the orange juice over and sprinkle lightly with salt and pepper. Cook, uncovered, for 1½ hours, basting twice with the juices.

2. Meanwhile cook the strips of orange zest in a small saucepan of boiling water for 5 minutes. Drain and set aside. In a cup, mix the cornflour to a paste with the cold water.

3. Remove the cooked lamb from the roasting tin and keep warm. Strain off any fat from the juices remaining in the tin, add the stock and stir in the cornflour paste. Bring to the boil, stirring constantly. Add the brandy, redcurrant jelly and reserved orange zest, with salt and pepper to taste. Lower the heat and simmer for about 2 minutes or until the jelly has melted.

4. Slice the lamb, arrange on a heated serving dish and spoon the sauce over. Sprinkle with the toasted flaked almonds and garnish with the parsley.

Cranberry-Stuffed Shoulder of Lamb

Serves: *6*

Preparation time: *15 minutes*

Cooking time: *2–2¼ hours*

Calories per portion: *485*

*1 boned shoulder of **New Zealand Lamb**, about 1.6 kg (3½ lb), trimmed*

3 satsumas

100 g (4 oz) caster sugar

350 g (12 oz) fresh or frozen cranberries

150 ml (¼ pint) water

25 g (1 oz) margarine

1 small onion, chopped finely

50 g (2 oz) medium oatmeal

125 ml (4 fl oz) chicken stock

salt and pepper

1 tbsp granulated sugar

parsley sprigs to garnish

1. Working over a strainer set over a saucepan, cut the satsumas in half and use a teaspoon to scrape out the flesh. Chop the satsuma flesh finely and set aside, with the satsuma shells.

2. Add half the chopped satsumas to the juice in

the saucepan. Stir in the caster sugar. Add half the cranberries, with the water. Bring to the boil, stirring occasionally, then cook over moderate heat for 10 minutes. Set aside to cool.

3. Melt the margarine in a saucepan, add the onion and fry gently for 2 minutes until soft. Stir in the oatmeal, stock, salt and pepper and granulated sugar. Add the remaining cranberries and chopped satsumas. Bring to the boil, stirring, then lower the heat and simmer for 2 minutes. Set aside to cool.

4. Set the oven at 190°C/375°F/Gas Mark 5. Place the lamb on a board, boned side uppermost. Fill the pocket of the lamb with the oatmeal stuffing. Close with a needle and fine string, or use skewers.

5. Place the lamb in a roasting tin and cook for 1¾ –2 hours until tender.

6. Fill each satsuma shell with cranberry sauce. Place the lamb on a heated serving dish, removing the string or skewers. Garnish with cranberry-filled satsuma shells and sprigs of parsley.

Cranberry-Stuffed Shoulder of Lamb

Gingered Honey Lamb

Serves: *6*

Preparation time:
5 minutes

Cooking time:
1¾ hours

Calories per portion: *280*

1 leg of **New Zealand Lamb**, *about 1.8 kg (4 lb),
trimmed*

2 tbsp lemon juice
2 tbsp clear honey
25 g (1 oz) fresh root ginger, peeled and grated
2 tablespoons chopped rosemary
2 kiwi fruit, peeled and sliced
rosemary sprigs to garnish

1. Set the oven at 190°C/375°F/Gas Mark 5. Using a sharp knife, score the surface of the lamb and place in a roasting tin.
2. Place the lemon juice and honey in separate bowls. Add half the ginger and rosemary to each bowl and mix well.
3. Brush the surface of the lamb with the lemon juice, ginger and rosemary mixture until evenly coated. Roast for 1¼ hours, then remove the

Gingered Honey Lamb

roasting tin from the oven.

4. Spread the honey, ginger and rosemary mixture evenly over the surface of the lamb and return to the oven for 20–30 minutes more. The lamb should be golden-brown and tender.

5. Transfer the lamb to a warmed serving plate. Garnish with the kiwi fruit slices and rosemary sprigs.

Lamb with Walnut and Basil Stuffing

Serves: *4*

Preparation time: *about 30 minutes*

Cooking time: *1¼ hours*

Calories per portion: *595*

Pictured on the front cover

*½ boned shoulder of **New Zealand Lamb** (blade half), about 1 kg (2¼ lb)*

1 tbsp oil
basil leaves or parsley sprigs to garnish
Stuffing:
1 onion, chopped
1 tbsp chopped fresh basil or ¾ tsp dried basil
1 tbsp grated lemon zest
40 g (1½ oz) shelled walnuts, chopped
salt and pepper
2 slices white or brown bread, crusts removed
6 tbsp milk
1 egg yolk
Tomato sauce:
425 g (15 oz) can of tomatoes
1 garlic clove, crushed
a good dash of Worcestershire sauce
a pinch of sugar
1 tsp chopped fresh basil or ½ tsp dried basil

1. Set the oven at 200°C/400°F/Gas Mark 6. Open up the lamb and remove any excess fat.

2. Make the stuffing. Cook the onion in a small saucepan of boiling water for 3–4 minutes, then drain thoroughly. Put the onion into a bowl with the basil, lemon zest and walnuts. Add salt and pepper to taste and mix well.

3. Soak the bread in the milk, squeeze out the excess, and crumble the bread into the stuffing ingredients. Mix well and bind with the egg yolk, adding a little of the soaking milk if necessary.

4. Spread the stuffing over one piece of the lamb and roll up or fold over to enclose. Close with a needle and fine string, or use skewers. Stand in a roasting tin. Brush lightly with the oil and roast for about 1¼ hours, until cooked through and well browned, basting at least once. Remove to a heated serving platter and keep warm. Pour off the fat from the roasting tin, leaving the juices.

5. Make the sauce. Purée the tomatoes with their juices in a blender or food processor. Add the purée to the roasting tin, with the garlic, Worcestershire sauce, sugar and basil. Bring to the boil, stirring frequently, and cook for 3–4 minutes. Adjust the seasonings.

6. Garnish the lamb with the basil or parsley. Serve with savoury rice, if liked.

Benmore Lamb

Serves: *8*

Preparation time: *20 minutes*

Cooking time: *2–2½ hours*

Calories per portion: *560*

*1 leg of **New Zealand Lamb**, about 2.25 kg (5 lb), trimmed*

2 garlic cloves, cut into thin slivers
1 sprig of fresh rosemary, plus extra to garnish
1.1 kg (2½ lb) potatoes, peeled and sliced thinly
2 onions, sliced thickly
salt and pepper
600 ml (1 pint) lamb or vegetable stock
Gravy:
1 tbsp plain flour
1 tbsp redcurrant jelly

1. Set the oven at 180°C/350°F/Gas Mark 4.
2. Using a sharp knife, make cuts in the meat and press a sliver of garlic into each. Tie the rosemary to the lamb bone with string. Put the lamb on a trivet in a roasting tin.
3. Layer the potatoes and onions in a large oven-proof dish, sprinkling salt and pepper between the layers. Pour over half the stock. Cover with foil.
4. Roast the lamb, basting two or three times with the cooking juices, for 2–2½ hours. The potatoes

and onions will require 1½ hours, so put them in the oven at the appropriate time, removing the foil for the final 30 minutes.

5. When the lamb is golden-brown and tender, transfer it to a serving dish and keep warm. Pour off and reserve the excess fat from the roasting tin.

6. Make the gravy by sprinkling the flour into the juices remaining in the tin. Cook over gentle heat until light brown. Stir in the remaining stock, bring to the boil, lower the heat and simmer for 5 minutes, stirring frequently. Stir in the redcurrant jelly, with salt and pepper to taste.

7. Brush the tops of the potatoes with the reserved lamb dripping and grill under moderate heat until brown. Garnish the lamb with rosemary and serve with the potato bake.

Launceston Lamb

Serves: *6*

Preparation time: *about 20 minutes*

Cooking time: *about 1¾ hours*

Calories per portion: *680*

1 shoulder of **New Zealand Lamb**, *about 1.5 kg (3¼ lb)*

1 garlic clove, crushed
salt and pepper
225 g (8 oz) carrots, sliced
1 aubergine, diced
2 onions, sliced
1 red pepper, cored, de-seeded and sliced
675 g (1½ lb) potatoes, peeled and sliced
400 ml (14 fl oz) lamb or vegetable stock
1 tbsp tomato purée
1 tbsp soy sauce
oil for greasing
parsley sprigs to garnish

1. Set the oven at 220°C/425°F/Gas Mark 7. Rub the lamb all over with the garlic. Sprinkle lightly with salt and pepper and stand in a lightly greased roasting tin.

2. Mix the carrots, aubergine, onions and pepper in a bowl. Layer the mixture, with the sliced potatoes, around the lamb.

3. Bring the stock to the boil in a saucepan. Add the tomato sauce, soy sauce and any remaining garlic, with plenty of salt and pepper. Pour over the lamb and vegetables.

4. Cover tightly with foil and cook for 1 hour. (If the joint is larger than 1.4 kg (3½ lb), allow 15 minutes more.)

5. Remove the foil and return the lamb to the oven for 30–45 minutes or until well browned and tender.

6. Transfer the lamb to a serving dish and garnish with parsley. Drain the vegetables, reserving the juices in a jug. Place some of the vegetables around the joint and put the rest in a serving dish. Skim off any fat from the surface of the juices and serve with the joint.

Children's Choice

Try a little tenderness next time you cook for the growing generation. New Zealand Lamb is the obvious choice for children. Succulent, tasty and nutritious, it's a treat they'll come back for again and again. In this chapter you'll find a host of new recipe ideas, from crunchy peanut burgers to a meat loaf hidden in a loaf of bread.

Okay Kebabs

Serves: *4*

Preparation time: *20 minutes + marinating*

Cooking time: *20–25 minutes*

Calories per portion: *345*

450 g (1 lb) **New Zealand Lamb** *fillet half of leg, trimmed and cut into 2.5 cm (1-inch) cubes*

1 red pepper, cored, de-seeded and cut into 2.5 cm (1-inch) pieces

1 green pepper, cored, de-seeded and cut into 2.5 cm (1-inch) pieces

8 cocktail sausages

Marinade:

1 tsp mild mustard
2 tbsp honey
2 tbsp sugar
grated zest and juice of 1 orange
salt and pepper

1. Thread the lamb, peppers and sausages alternately on to 4 skewers. Place side by side in a shallow dish.
2. Make the marinade by mixing all the ingredients together in a jug. Pour over the kebabs, cover and marinate in a cool place for at least 2 hours.
3. Drain the kebabs, reserving the marinade. Grill under moderate heat for 20–25 minutes, basting with the reserved marinade and turning once.
4. Serve with rice, tomatoes and slices of orange, if liked.

Surprise Lamb Loaf

Serves: 6

Preparation time:
10 minutes

Cooking time:
30 minutes

Calories per portion: *330*

*450 g (1 lb) minced **New Zealand Lamb***
1 onion, chopped finely
½ red pepper, cored, de-seeded and finely chopped
175 g (6 oz) mushrooms, finely chopped
227 g (8 oz) can tomatoes
2 tbsp tomato purée
salt and pepper
½ tsp dried basil
1 round loaf of white or granary bread
25 g (1 oz) Cheddar cheese, grated

1. Combine the lamb and onion in a heavy-bottomed saucepan. Heat gently until the fat runs, then raise the heat and fry until the lamb is browned. Add the red pepper and mushrooms.
2. Using a sharp knife, cut up the tomatoes in the can, then tip the tomatoes and the can juices into the saucepan. Stir in the tomato purée, salt, pepper and basil. Bring the mixture to the boil, then lower the heat and simmer for 20 minutes, stirring occasionally. Set aside to cool.
3. Set the oven at 180°C/350°F/Gas Mark 4. Place the loaf upside down on a board and carefully cut a circle, about 10 cm (4 inches) in diameter, from the base. Set the bread circle aside, then carefully scoop out most of the centre of the loaf.
4. Crumb the bread in a food processor or on a grater. Add 6 tbsp of the crumbs to the lamb mixture, reserving the remainder for use in a another dish. Mix well, then spoon the filling into the hollowed loaf. Replace the bread circle, cover the loaf with a large piece of foil and carefully invert loaf and foil on to a baking sheet.
5. Sprinkle the top of the loaf with the cheese and bring the sides of the foil up to enclose it. Transfer the loaf to the oven and bake for 20 minutes or until the filling is hot and the cheese topping has melted.
6. Unwrap the loaf, taking care not to dislodge the 'plug' in the base. Place on a plate and cut in wedges.

Lamburgers with Peanuts

Serves: *4*

Preparation time: *10 minutes*

Cooking time: *6–8 minutes*

Calories per portion: *460*

*450 g (1 lb) minced **New Zealand Lamb***
1 onion, chopped finely or minced
40 g (1½ oz) roasted or salted peanuts, chopped finely
½ tsp dried mixed herbs
salt and pepper
4 hamburger buns
Garnish:
2–3 tbsp crunchy or smooth peanut butter
2 tomatoes, sliced
parsley sprigs

1. Mix the lamb, onion, peanuts and herbs in a bowl with salt and pepper to taste. Bind together and divide into 4. Shape into round burgers.
2. Cook the burgers on a rack under a moderate grill for 6–8 minutes, turning once.
3. Meanwhile, split the buns and toast the cut sides. When the burgers are cooked, place one on each bun base.
4. Shape the peanut butter into 8 small balls. Use to garnish the burgers, with tomato slices and parsley sprigs. Replace the lids of the buns and serve at once.

Lamburgers with Peanuts

South Island Surprise

Serves: *2*

Preparation time: *10 minutes*

Cooking time: *20 minutes*

Calories per portion: *388*

*100 g (4 oz) cooked **New Zealand Lamb** shoulder, trimmed and cubed*

40 g (1½ oz) plain flour
salt and pepper
150 ml (¼ pint) milk
1 egg (size 3)
½ tsp dried mixed herbs
½ onion, chopped finely
2 tsp oil
2 tbsp peas
2 tbsp sweetcorn
Topping:
1 tomato, sliced
25 g (1 oz) grated cheese

1. Preheat the oven to 180°C/350°F/Gas Mark 4. Whisk the flour and seasoning with the milk and egg until smooth. Bring to the boil on a gentle heat, stirring constantly, until thickened. Add the herbs and the cubed lamb.

2. Cook the onion in the oil until tender. Divide between 2 shallow ovenproof dishes. Divide the peas and sweecorn between the dishes and spoon over the lamb mixture.

South Island Surprise

3. Cook in the oven for 15–20 minutes, until golden-brown and just set.

4. Make the topping by covering each dish with sliced tomato and grated cheese. Grill the topping under a preheated grill until golden and bubbling.

Lamb and Cranberry Flips

Serves: 6

Preparation time:
15 minutes

Cooking time:
10 minutes

Calories per portion: *295*

*225 g (8 oz) cooked **New Zealand Lamb**, trimmed and cut into 1 cm (½ -inch) cubes*

15 g (½ oz) butter
1 onion, chopped finely
100 g (4 oz) mushrooms, sliced
1 tbsp plain flour
100 g (4 oz) cranberry jelly plus extra to serve
150 ml (¼ pint) lamb or vegetable stock
salt and pepper
parsley sprigs to garnish
Pancakes:
100 g (4 oz) plain flour
a pinch of salt
1 egg plus 1 egg yolk
300 ml (½ pint) milk
1 tbsp oil, plus extra for frying
3 tbsp grated parmesan cheese

1. Make the pancake batter. Combine the flour and salt in a large bowl. Stir in the egg and extra yolk. Gradually beat in the milk to form a smooth batter. Add the oil and half the cheese. Pour the batter into a jug.

2. Lightly grease a 20 cm (8-inch) pancake pan with oil and place over moderate heat. When the pan is hot, pour in enough batter to cover the base of the pan with a thin film. Cook until bubbles form, then flip over to cook the other side. Make 5 more pancakes in the same way. Stack the cooked pancakes on a plate over a saucepan of simmering water to keep warm.

3. To make the filling, melt the butter in a saucepan, add the onion and fry gently for 3 minutes until soft. Add the mushrooms and cook over high heat, stirring, for 2 minutes. Stir in the flour, jelly, stock and lamb, with salt and pepper to taste. Simmer gently for 5–10 minutes.

4. Divide the filling between the pancakes and fold up. Lay the filled pancakes in a buttered dish. Sprinkle the remaining cheese over the top. Brown under a moderate grill.

5. Garnish with parsley and serve with more cranberry sauce.

New Zealand Lamb Tacos

Serves: *8*

Preparation time:
10 minutes

Cooking time:
20 minutes

Calories per portion: *245*

Pictured on the back cover

*450 g (1 lb) minced **New Zealand Lamb***
1 tbsp oil
1 onion, chopped
1 garlic clove, crushed (optional)
1 tbsp mild chilli powder
1 tsp ground coriander
227 g (8 oz) can of tomatoes
1 tbsp tomato purée
275 g (10 oz) can red kidney beans, drained
8 taco shells
Garnish:
crisp lettuce, shredded
spring onions, topped, tailed and diced
grated Cheddar cheese

1. Heat the oil in a large pan. Add the onion, garlic (if used), chilli powder and coriander. Fry gently for 2–3 minutes until the onion is soft.

2. Add the lamb and fry until brown. Stir in the tomatoes and tomato purée. Lower the heat and simmer for 20 minutes until the liquid has reduced. Stir occasionally to prevent sticking.

3. Set the oven at 180°C/350°F/Gas Mark 4. Add the kidney beans to the lamb mixture and heat thoroughly.

4. Heat the taco shells in the oven for 3 minutes. Put one taco shell on each plate and divide the meat mixture between them. Top with lettuce, spring onions and cheese and serve immediately.

Mini Meatball Pittas

Serves: *6*

Preparation time:
10 minutes

Cooking time:
5 minutes

Calories per portion: *170*

Mini Meatball Pittas

225 g (8 oz) minced or chopped **New Zealand Lamb**

grated zest of 1 lemon
salt and pepper
1 tsp ground cumin
3 pitta breads
Salad garnish:
3 carrots, grated
7.5 cm (3-inch) piece of cucumber, diced
3 tomatoes, diced
1 tbsp chopped fresh herbs (optional)
3 tbsp plain yogurt

1. In a large bowl, mix the lamb with the lemon zest. Add ½ tsp salt, pepper to taste and cumin. Form into 18 small meatballs.

2. Place the meatballs in a grill pan and grill under moderate heat for 5 minutes, turning once.

3. Make the salad garnish by mixing the grated carrot, cucumber, tomatoes, herbs (if used) and yogurt. Add salt and pepper to taste.

4. Cut the pitta breads in half. Gently ease each half open to form a pocket. Fill each pitta pocket with 3 mini meatballs and a portion of salad garnish. Serve at once.

Crunchy Riblets

Serves: *4*

Preparation time: *5 minutes*

Cooking time: *25–30 minutes*

Calories per portion: *720*

*16 breast riblets of **New Zealand Lamb**, trimmed*

2 eggs
2 tbsp water
1 tsp dried oregano
100 g (4 oz) porridge oats
1 tsp salt
parsley to garnish
tomato ketchup to serve

1. Set the oven at 200°C/400°F/Gas Mark 6. Beat the eggs with the water in a shallow bowl. Mix the oregano, oats and salt on a piece of greaseproof paper.

2. Coat the riblets, one at a time, first in egg and then in oats. Use the paper to press the oats firmly on to the meat.

3. Place the coated riblets on a baking sheet and bake for 25–30 minutes until browned.

4. Drain the riblets. Serve hot or cold, garnished with parsley and with a dipping sauce of tomato ketchup.

Lampasta

Serves: *8*

Preparation time:
20 minutes

Cooking time:
1½–2 hours

Calories per portion: *505*

*450 g (1 lb) minced **New Zealand Lamb***
225 g (8 oz) brown lentils, soaked and drained
450 g (1 lb) wholewheat short-cut macaroni
salt and pepper
2 onions, chopped finely
1 garlic clove, crushed
397 g (14 oz) can of chopped tomatoes
3 tbsp tomato purée
½ tsp dried oregano
butter for greasing
Topping:
300 ml (½ pint) plain yogurt
1 egg
225 g (8 oz) low-fat cottage cheese
a pinch of grated nutmeg
3–4 tbsp grated parmesan cheese

1. Bring a saucepan of water to the boil. Add the lentils and cook for 20 minutes until almost tender. Do not add salt. Drain the cooked lentils and set aside.
2. Cook the macaroni in a saucepan of boiling salted water for 12 minutes. Drain well.
3. Put the lamb into a heavy-bottomed saucepan and heat gently until the fat starts to run. Raise the heat and cook until the lamb is well sealed, stirring from time to time. With a slotted spoon, transfer the lamb to a bowl and set aside. Pour off all but 2 tbsp of the fat from the pan.
4. Add the onions and garlic to the fat remaining in the pan and fry for 3 minutes, stirring frequently. Add the lentils, lamb and tomatoes, with their juices. Stir in the tomato purée and oregano, with salt and pepper to taste. Bring to the boil, lower the heat, cover and simmer for 30 minutes.
5. Set the oven at 200°C/400°F/Gas Mark 6. Put half the macaroni in a greased baking dish and cover with half the lamb sauce. Repeat the layers.
6. Make the topping by mixing the yogurt, egg,

cottage cheese and nutmeg in a bowl. Beat until
well mixed. Add salt and pepper to taste, then
pour over the layers in the dish. Sprinkle the
cheese over the top.

7. Bake for 30 minutes. Serve hot.

Wellington Shepherd's Pie

Serves: *4*

Preparation time:
10–15 minutes

Cooking time:
1¼ hours

Calories per portion: *620*

450 g (1 lb) minced **New Zealand Lamb**

1 onion, chopped finely
300 ml (½ pint) lamb stock
900 g (2 lb) potatoes, peeled and halved
salt and pepper
1 tbsp cornflour
50 g (2 oz) butter
432 g (15 oz) can of red kidney beans, drained
150 ml (¼ pint) milk

1. Fry the lamb until the fat starts to run.

2. Add the onion and stir until lightly browned all
over. Add the stock, cover and simmer for 30
minutes.

3. Meanwhile, cook the potatoes in a saucepan of
boiling salted water for 25–30 minutes or until
tender.

4. Set the oven at 180°C/350°F/Gas Mark 4.
Remove the lamb from the heat and let stand for
5 minutes. Skim off any fat, then add salt and
pepper to taste. In a cup, mix the cornflour to a
paste with a little water.

5. Return the lamb to the heat, stir in the
cornflour mixture and bring to the boil. Stir in the
kidney beans and spoon into a pie dish. Cool.

6. Drain the potatoes. Mash with 25 g (1 oz) of the
butter and the milk. Add salt and pepper to taste.

7. Spoon over the top of the lamb mixture, then
ridge up with a fork. Dot with the remaining
butter. Bake for 30 minutes until browned on top,
finishing under the grill if necessary.

Timaru Cutlets

Serves: *4*

Preparation time:
5 minutes

Cooking time:
12–14 minutes

Calories per portion: *260*

*4 **New Zealand Lamb** best end of neck cutlets or loin chops, trimmed*

1 tbsp oil

Quick tomato sauce:

4 tbsp tomato ketchup

1 tbsp honey or golden syrup

6 tbsp water or chicken stock

1. Put the cutlets on a rack over a grill pan. Brush lightly with the oil and cook under moderate heat for 6–7 minutes on each side.

2. Meanwhile make the sauce by gently warming all the ingredients in a saucepan until the honey has melted. Pour into a sauce boat.

3. Serve the cutlets with low-fat crisps and peas, if liked. Offer the sauce separately.

Special Occasions

Every meal is a special occasion with New Zealand lamb, but there are times – family celebrations, reunions with friends, dinners for business associates – when something extra-special is called for. The pages that follow are packed with entertaining ideas, some of them surprisingly economical and easy to cook.

Lamb Puffs

Makes: 24	
Preparation time: 25 minutes	
Cooking time: 25 minutes	
Calories per portion: 75	

100 g (4 oz) cooked **New Zealand Lamb**, chopped finely
65 g (2½ oz) butter
150 ml (¼ pint) water
65 g (2½ oz) plain flour
1 onion, chopped finely
2 streaky bacon rashers, rind removed, chopped finely
salt and pepper
1 tsp dried dill weed
2 large eggs, beaten
1 tbsp grated parmesan cheese
oil for deep frying
celery leaves to garnish
Sauce:
150 ml (¼ pint) plain yogurt
½ cucumber, with peel, grated coarsely
1 tbsp snipped chives or chopped spring onions

1. Make the sauce by combining the yogurt, cucumber and chives or spring onions in a bowl. Add salt and pepper to taste, mix well and set aside.
2. Put 50 g (2 oz) of the butter in a saucepan with the water. Heat gently until the butter melts, then bring to the boil. Add the flour all at once. Beat the mixture until it is smooth and thick, and leaves the sides of the pan clean. Remove from the heat, spread the paste over the base of the

saucepan and leave to cool.

3. Melt the remaining butter in a frying-pan and fry the onion, bacon and lamb until the onion is golden and the bacon has begun to crisp. Stir frequently. Season with plenty of salt and pepper, add the dill and set aside to cool.

4. Using an electric whisk, gradually beat the eggs into the paste until smooth and glossy, then beat in the parmesan cheese. Drain the lamb mixture thoroughly and stir it into the paste.

5. Heat the oil in a deep fat-fryer to 180–190°C/350-375°F or until a cube of bread added to the oil browns in 30 seconds. Carefully add teaspoons of the lamb mixture to the oil, about 6 at a time. Fry until golden, then turn the puffs with a slotted spoon and continue frying until well browned.

6. Drain the puffs on absorbent kitchen paper and keep warm while frying the remainder. Serve the puffs with the sauce with pre-dinner drinks or as a starter.

Guard of Honour with Leek and Courgette Stuffing

Serves: *6*

Preparation time: *about 30 minutes*

Cooking time: *about 1¾ hours*

Calories per portion: *610*

*2 best ends of **New Zealand Lamb**, chined*
1 tbsp oil
675 g (1½ lb) potatoes, peeled
40 g (1½ oz) almonds, toasted and chopped
1 egg, beaten
Stuffing:
25 g (1 oz) butter
1 leek, about 75 g (3 oz), sliced thinly
1 garlic clove, crushed
175 g (6 oz) courgettes, grated coarsely
½ teaspoon dried basil or tarragon
75 g (3 oz) soft white or brown breadcrumbs
salt and pepper
1 egg, beaten
Garnish:
baby sweetcorn
parsley

1. Trim 2.5 cm (1 inch) from the ends of the rib bones. (Given a few days' notice, your butcher will do this.) Set the oven at 200°C/400°F/Gas Mark 6.

2. Make the stuffing. Melt the butter in a saucepan, add the leek and garlic and fry very gently for about 5 minutes until soft. Add the courgettes and cook for 3–4 minutes. When the courgettes are soft, tip the vegetables into a bowl. Set aside to cool.

3. Add the herbs and breadcrumbs to the vegetable mixture; season to taste. Bind with the egg.

4. Stand both joints of meat together in a roasting tin with the bone tips crossed like swords. Put the stuffing into the centre of the lamb. Protect the bone tips with foil. Brush the meat with the oil and roast for about 1½ hours.

5. Meanwhile cook the potatoes in boiling salted water. Sieve the potatoes into a bowl and beat in the nuts and egg, with salt and pepper to taste. Put into a piping bag with a large nozzle and pipe a potato surround for the lamb on a large ovenproof plate. Put the plate into the oven below the lamb for the last 30 minutes of cooking time.

6. When the lamb is cooked but still pink, place it in the centre of the piped potato border. Replace the foil on the bone ends with cutlet frills. Serve garnished with baby sweetcorn and parsley.

Dunedin Lamb and Apricot Casserole

Serves: *6*

Preparation time:
20 minutes, plus soaking

Cooking time:
45 minutes

Calories per portion: *310*

*1 boned shoulder of **New Zealand Lamb**, about 1.4 kg (3 lb), trimmed and cut into 2.5 cm (1-inch) cubes*

175 g (6 oz) dried apricots, soaked overnight
2 tbsp oil
2 onions, chopped
½ tsp ground cinnamon
a pinch of ground ginger
450 ml (¾ pint) lamb or vegetable stock
salt and pepper
parsley to garnish

1. Drain the apricots, reserving 2 tbsp of the soaking liquor. Set half the apricots aside. Purée the remainder with the reserved soaking liquid in a food processor or by pressing through a sieve into a bowl.

2. Heat the oil in a large flameproof casserole, add the onions and fry until soft. Add the lamb and fry until evenly browned.

3. Pour off the excess fat from the pan and add the cinnamon, ginger, apricot purée, whole apricots and stock, with salt and pepper to taste.

4. Bring to the boil, then lower the heat, cover and simmer for about 45 minutes or until the lamb is tender.

5. Stir the casserole, taste and adjust the seasoning if necessary.

6. Garnish with parsley and serve at once, with boiled rice or noodles and crisp green beans, if liked.

Dunedin Lamb and Apricot Casserole

Lamb Filo Parcels

Serves: *4*

Preparation time:
30 minutes

Cooking time:
1 hour

Calories per portion: *1210*

4 **New Zealand Lamb** *double loin chops, trimmed*

100 g (4 oz) butter

1 tbsp dried tarragon

1 tbsp dried basil

1 tbsp dried oregano

24 sheets of filo pastry

50 g (2 oz) soft white or brown breadcrumbs

4 tbsp dried mushroom slices

100 g (4 oz) Mozzarella cheese, sliced

2 tomatoes, sliced thickly

1. Melt the butter in a small saucepan and stir in the herbs. Cut 4 strips, each 2.5 cm (1 inch) wide, from the long side of 4 sheets of filo. Form the strips into rosettes and wrap in cling film, so that they do not dry out. Stack the remaining filo under a dry tea towel, with a dampened tea towel on top.

Lamb Filo Parcels

2. Set the oven at 190°C/375°F/Gas Mark 5. Mix the breadcrumbs and mushrooms in a bowl.

3. Layer 6 sheets of pastry, brushing each layer with herb butter and using one of the cut sheets as the top layer. Place a quarter of the breadcrumb mixture in the centre of the top sheet of pastry and arrange a double chop on top. Top with a quarter of the Mozzarella cheese and a quarter of the tomato slices. Draw up the sides of the pastry and seal to make a neat parcel. Garnish with a filo rosette.

4. Make 3 more parcels in the same way, keeping any unused filo and the prepared filo parcels under tea towels to prevent them from drying out.

5. Place the parcels on a baking sheet and bake for about 1 hour. Serve at once.

Kiwi Lamb and Kidney Nests

Serves: *4*

Preparation time:
20 minutes plus chilling

Cooking time:
about 40 minutes

Calories per portion: *530*

*1 **New Zealand Lamb** best end of neck*
2 New Zealand Lamb kidneys
675 g (1½ lb) potatoes, peeled
25 g (1 oz) butter
1 egg yolk
a little milk
Garnish:
4 short streaky bacon rashers
4 stuffed olives

1. Remove the bone from the best end of neck, then lay whole or halved lamb's kidneys along the length of the joint. Roll up to enclose the kidney. Secure with string or skewers and chill.

2. When required, cut the lamb roll into 4 equal slices. Put a cocktail stick through each to maintain the shape during cooking.

3. Cook the potatoes in boiling salted water until tender. Drain thoroughly, then sieve until very smooth. Beat in the butter, egg yolk and enough milk to give a piping consistency.

4. Put the potato into a piping bag fitted with a star vegetable nozzle and pipe four nests on to greased foil. Alternatively, make the nests by shaping with a fork. Place in a grill pan and cook under moderate heat, turning once, until beginning to brown. Remove and keep hot.

5. Put the lamb and kidney rolls into the grill pan. Cook under moderate heat for about 10 minutes or until well browned and cooked through.

6. Meanwhile stretch each bacon rasher over the back of a knife and cut in half lengthways. Make 8 bacon rolls. Put 2 bacon rolls and 1 olive on each of 4 wooden cocktail sticks. Add to the grill pan for the last 4-5 minutes of cooking.

7. To serve, put each potato nest on a warmed plate. Remove the wooden cocktail sticks from the lamb rolls and place 1 roll in the centre of each nest. Garnish with the bacon kebabs. Serve with a fresh green salad, if liked.

Ginger and Orange Lamb Steaks

Serves: *4*

Preparation time: *5 minutes*

Cooking time: *25 minutes*

Calories per portion: *380*

*4 **New Zealand Lamb** leg bone steaks, trimmed*
150 ml (¼ pint) ginger wine
grated zest and juice of 1 orange
4 cloves
1 tbsp chopped crystallised ginger
1 tbsp chopped fresh mint
2 tsp cornflour
Garnish:
fresh mint leaves
orange slices
strips of crystallised ginger

1. Fry the steaks quickly in a large ungreased frying-pan until sealed on both sides.

2. Add the ginger wine, orange zest and juice, cloves, crystallised ginger and mint. Bring the sauce to the boil, then lower the heat, cover the pan and simmer for 20 minutes until the lamb is tender.

3. Transfer the lamb steaks to a heated serving dish and keep warm.

4. In a cup, blend the cornflour with a little water to make a smooth paste. Stir the paste into the sauce. Stirring constantly, bring to the boil, then lower the heat and simmer until the sauce thickens.

5. Spoon the sauce over the lamb steaks. Garnish with mint leaves, orange slices and ginger and serve at once.

Ginger and Orange Lamb Steaks

Kiwi Glazed Lamb

Serves: *6*

Preparation time:
25 minutes

Cooking time:
1¾ hours

Calories per portion: *295*

*1 leg of **New Zealand Lamb**, about 1.6 kg
(3½ lb), trimmed*
3 ripe kiwi fruit
4 tsp soft light brown sugar
4 tsp lime or lemon juice
300 ml (½ pint) water
2 tsp cornflour
2 tsp soy sauce
Garnish:
mint sprigs
lime slices

1. Set the oven at 180°C/350°F/Gas Mark 4. Place the lamb on a rack in a roasting tin.
2. Peel and chop 1 kiwi fruit. Purée it in a blender or food processor with 1 tbsp of the sugar and 1 tbsp of the lime juice.
3. With a sharp knife, makes small slashes in the lamb at intervals. Spread the kiwi fruit mixture evenly over the surface. Pour the water into the

Kiwi Glazed Lamb

roasting tin below the lamb and roast for 35 minutes per 450 g (1 lb). Cover with foil if the lamb starts to become too brown.

4. Transfer the lamb to a serving dish and keep warm. Pour the juices from the tin into a measuring jug, skim off the fat and make the juices up to 300 ml (½ pint) with water. Pour the mixture back into the roasting tin.

5. In a small bowl, blend the cornflour and remaining sugar with the remaining lime juice and the soy sauce. Tip the mixture into the roasting tin. Bring to the boil, stirring until the sauce is smooth and thick. Peel and chop 1 kiwi fruit and stir it into the sauce. Season to taste with salt and pepper and pour into a sauce boat.

6. Peel and slice the remaining kiwi fruit and arrange over the lamb. Serve with the hot sauce and garnish with mint sprigs and lime slices.

Milford Sound Lamb with Whisky

Serves: *4*

Preparation time: *10 minutes*

Cooking time: *25 minutes*

Calories per portion: *355*

575 g (1¼ lb) **New Zealand Lamb** *fillet, trimmed and cut into strips*

25 g (1 oz) butter or margarine

1 tbsp oil

1 onion, sliced thinly

1 garlic clove, crushed

2 tbsp whisky

150 ml (¼ pint) lamb or vegetable stock

salt and pepper

150 ml (¼ pint) soured cream

2 tbsp snipped chives or chopped parsley to garnish

1. Heat the fat and the oil in a large frying-pan. Add the onion and garlic and fry gently for 4–5 minutes until soft.

2. Add the lamb and continue to fry until it is well sealed all over.

3. Pour the whisky over the lamb and ignite, then add the stock, with salt and pepper to taste. Bring to the boil, lower the heat, cover and simmer gently for 10 minutes.

4. Stir in the soured cream and reheat gently. Adjust the seasoning and sprinkle with chives or parsley. Serve at once, with buttered noodles or creamed potatoes, if liked.

Conway Lamb Cutlets with Spiced Fruit

Serves: *4*

Preparation time: *5 minutes*

Cooking time: *15–20 minutes*

Calories per portion: *420*

8 *New Zealand Lamb* cutlets, trimmed

parsley sprigs to garnish

Sauce:

2 tbsp soft light brown sugar
2 tbsp white wine vinegar
1 tbsp lemon juice
250 ml (8 fl oz) lamb or vegetable stock
½ tsp ground allspice
12 no-need-to-soak prunes
salt and pepper
2 eating apples
1 tsp cornflour

1. Make the sauce. Heat the brown sugar gently in the top of a double saucepan until it starts to melt and caramelise. Quickly add the vinegar, lemon juice, stock and allspice. Bring to the boil.

2. Add the prunes, with salt and pepper to taste. Lower the heat and simmer for 4–5 minutes.

3. Peel, core and slice the apples and add to the pan. Poach gently until soft but not broken up.

4. Meanwhile put the cornflour in a cup and blend with enough water to form a smooth paste. Stir into the sauce. Bring back to the boil until thickened, then place the pan over gently steaming water to keep the sauce warm.

5. Grill the cutlets under moderate heat for 5–7 minutes on each side until well browned and cooked through.

6. Place a cutlet frill on each bone end. Arrange the cutlets on a heated platter and spoon the sauce around them. Garnish with parsley and serve at once.

Cidered Lamb and Apple Pie

Serves: *6*

Preparation time:
25 minutes

Cooking time:
1 hour

Calories per portion: *430*

*½ leg of **New Zealand Lamb** (fillet end), about 800 g (1¾ lb), trimmed and cubed*

225 g (8 oz) cooking apples
25 g (1 oz) soft light brown sugar
1 tbsp plain flour
¼ tsp ground cinnamon
¼ tsp ground allspice
salt and pepper
1 large onion, sliced
150 ml (¼ pint) cider

Pastry:
175 g (6 oz) plain flour
½ tsp salt
50 g (2 oz) butter or margarine
25 g (1 oz) lard
1–2 tbsp cold water
beaten egg or milk to glaze

1. Set the oven at 200°C/400°F/Gas Mark 6. Peel, core and slice the apples. Mix the sugar, flour, spices, salt and pepper in a bowl.

2. Arrange half the onion and apple slices on the base of a 1.2–litre (2-pint) pie dish. Place the lamb cubes on the top and sprinkle with the flour mixture. Top with the remaining onion and apple. Pour over the cider.

3. To make the pastry, place the flour and the salt in a mixing bowl. Rub in the fats until the mixture resembles fine breadcrumbs. Add enough water to make a firm dough.

4. Roll out the pastry on a floured board and cover the pie. Roll out the trimmings, cut into long thin strips and use to make a lattice design on the top crust. Brush with egg or milk. Make a small hole in the centre of the pie to act as a steam vent.

5. Bake for 30 minutes, then lower the oven temperature to 180°C/350°F/Gas Mark 4 and bake for 30 minutes more. Cover the pie with greaseproof paper if the top crust starts to brown too much. Serve hot.

Outward Bound

When you are bound for the great outdoors, whether for a barbecue in the garden or a picnic by the edge of the sea, make sure you pack plenty of lamb. The recipes in this section have been selected for their variety and versatility. All are easy to prepare and simple to serve, from cutlets that come in a handy toast wrapper to a portable picnic stew.

Alfresco Lamb Loaf

Makes: *8 slices*

Preparation time: *30 minutes*

Cooking time: *1¼ hours*

Calories per portion: *190*

*675 g (1½ lb) boned shoulder of **New Zealand Lamb**, trimmed and cut into 2.5 cm (1-inch) cubes*
50 g (2 oz) natural bran
225 g (8 oz) potato, peeled and grated
1 onion, grated
1 garlic clove, crushed
1 tsp dried mixed herbs
1 tsp ground coriander
6 tbsp tomato ketchup
1 tsp salt
pepper
2 tbsp gravy granules or powder
2 eggs
To garnish:
radish roses
cucumber slices
spring onions

1. Set the oven at 190°C/375°F/Gas Mark 5. Line a 450 g (1 lb) loaf tin with a strip of foil each way, leaving sufficient foil to fold over the top of the loaf.
2. Put the lamb cubes in a large bowl. Add all the remaining ingredients except the garnish and mix well. Spoon into the prepared tin and press down well. Fold the foil over the top, place the tin on a baking sheet and bake for 1¼ hours.
3. Place a weight (or a bag of sugar) on top of the cooked loaf and leave to cool in the tin. Remove the weight and chill the loaf in the refrigerator

until required. It will keep for a few days.

4. Turn out and serve or transport to the picnic in the tin. Garnish with radish roses, cucumber slices and spring onions, and serve in thick slices.

Picnic Pasties

Makes: *8*

Preparation time:
20 minutes + chilling

Cooking time:
45 minutes

Calories per portion: *440*

450 g (1 lb) diced shoulder of **New Zealand Lamb**

1 small turnip, chopped roughly (optional)
2 potatoes, peeled and diced
2 small onions, chopped finely
salt and pepper
a pinch of nutmeg
1 egg, beaten, to glaze
Pastry:
350 g (12 oz) plain flour
75 g (3 oz) butter
75 g (3 oz) vegetable fat
about 5 tbsp iced water

1. Make the pastry. Place the flour in the mixing bowl with 1/2 tsp salt. Rub in the fats until the mixture resembles fine breadcrumbs. Add enough of the iced water to make a firm dough. Wrap and chill for at least 30 minutes.

2. Set the oven at 200°C/400°F/ Gas Mark 6. Mix the lamb, turnip (if used), potatoes and onions in a bowl. Season generously with salt and pepper and add the nutmeg.

3. Roll out the pastry on a floured board. Using a saucer as a guide, cut out 8 rounds, gathering together the trimmings and re-rolling as required.

4. Place a small heap of the filling in the centre of a pastry round. Brush the edges of the pastry lightly with water, then fold the pastry over to form a semi-circle. Crimp the edges firmly together to seal. Make 7 more pasties in the same way.

5. Place the pasties on 2–3 baking sheets. Using a sharp knife, make two small slashes in the top crust of each to allow steam to escape, then brush with beaten egg to glaze.

6. Bake for 15 minutes, then lower the oven temperature to 180°C/350°F/Gas Mark 4 and bake for 30 minutes more or until deep golden in colour. If the pasties start to become too brown, cover them with foil.
7. Serve hot or cold, with fruit chutney, if liked.

Raised Lamb and Apricot Pie

Serves: *8*

Preparation time:
35 minutes

Cooking time:
2 hours

Calories per portion: *405*

450 g (1 lb) neck fillet of **New Zealand Lamb***, chined, chopped into small pieces (see Note)*
1 cm (½-inch) piece of root ginger, peeled and chopped finely
1 garlic clove, crushed
1 onion, chopped finely
2 tsp soy sauce
salt and pepper
100 g (4 oz) no-need-to-soak dried apricots
Pastry:
350 g (12 oz) plain flour, plus extra for rolling
1 tsp salt
150 g (5 oz) lard
150 ml (¼ pint) water
beaten egg to glaze

1. Place the lamb, ginger, garlic and onion in a bowl. Add the soy sauce with salt and pepper to taste. Mix well. Cover and leave to stand while making the pastry.
2. Sift the flour and salt into a mixing bowl. Place the lard and water in a small saucepan and heat gently until the lard has melted. Stir into the flour with a fork to make a soft dough. Cool the dough slightly, then knead until smooth.
3. Set the oven at 200°C/400°F/Gas Mark 6. Roll out two-thirds of the dough on a floured board and line a 900 g (2 lb) loaf tin. Press half the filling on to the base, then cover with the apricots. Spread the remaining filling over the top and smooth the surface.
4. Roll out the remaining pastry on a floured board to make a lid for the pie. Damp the edges and cover the pie, trimming off the excess pastry. Pinch

the join together with finger and thumb to seal and decorate. Roll out the trimmings and cut into shapes to decorate the top crust.

5. Brush the pie with beaten egg. Bake for 30 minutes, then lower the oven temperature to 180°C/350°F/Gas Mark 4 and bake for 1½ hours more. Cover the pie with greaseproof paper if it becomes too brown.

6. Cool the pie in the tin for 20 minutes. Turn out and serve or transport to the picnic in the tin. Serve warm or cold, with a selection of salads.

Note: The lamb, ginger, garlic and onion may all be chopped finely together in a food processor, if liked.

Raised Lamb and Apricot Pie

Butterflied Leg of Lamb

Serves: 6

Preparation time:
5 minutes + marinating

Cooking time:
1 hour

Calories per portion: 00

1 boned leg of **New Zealand Lamb**

Marinade:
300 ml (½ pint) white wine
300 ml (½ pint) oil
grated zest and juice of 3 lemons
2 garlic cloves, crushed
50 g (2 oz) soft light brown sugar
salt and pepper

1. Open the boned leg out flat to form a butterfly shape.
2. Combine all the ingredients for the marinade in a dish large enough to hold the butterflied leg.
3. Add the lamb to the dish, cover and marinate for at least 4 hours, preferably overnight. Turn the lamb over several times.
4. Remove the lamb, reserving the marinade, and pat dry with absorbent kitchen paper. Cook on a barbecue grill for about 1 hour, turning once and basting with the reserved marinade.

Clockwise:
Butterflied Leg of Lamb;
Summer Kebabs;
Barbecued
Leg Bone Steaks

Barbecued Leg Bone Steaks

Serves: *4*

Preparation time:
5 minutes + marinating

Cooking time:
30 minutes

Calories per portion: *335*

4 *New Zealand Lamb* leg bone steaks, trimmed
salt and pepper
Marinade:
2 tsp curry powder
1 onion, chopped finely
4 tbsp apple or pineapple juice
2 tbsp vinegar
1 tbsp oil
1 tbsp soft light brown sugar
a pinch of cinnamon

1. Combine all the marinade ingredients in a shallow dish large enough to hold all the steaks in a single layer.
2. Add the steaks, cover and marinate for at least 4 hours, preferably overnight.
3. Remove the lamb, reserving the marinade, and pat dry with absorbent kitchen paper. Cook on a barbecue grill for about 30 minutes, turning the steaks once and basting with the reserved marinade.

Summer Kebabs

Serves: *4*

Preparation time:
15 minutes + marinating

Cooking time:
12–15 minutes

Calories per kebab: *000*

375 g (12 oz) lean leg or shoulder of **New Zealand Lamb**
1 tbsp oil
1 tbsp wine vinegar
a pinch of dried mixed herbs
salt and pepper
½ onion, cut into 8
½ green or red pepper, de-seeded and cut into 8

1. Cut the lamb into 16 cubes. Mix the oil, vinegar, herbs and seasonings, and marinate the lamb in this mixture for several hours, or preferably overnight.
2. Drain the lamb and thread the cubes, with the onion and pepper pieces, on to 4 kebab sticks.
3. Grill until well browned, turning occasionally, for about 12 minutes.

Barbecue Burgers

Serves: *8*

Preparation time:
3 minutes

Cooking time:
15 minutes

Calories per portion: *305*

450 g (1 lb) minced **New Zealand Lamb**
25 g (1 oz) butter
1 onion, chopped finely
1 celery stick, chopped finely
1 tbsp tomato purée
1 tbsp tomato ketchup
1 tsp dried mixed herbs
salt and pepper
50 g (2 oz) soft white breadcrumbs
8 soft rolls, split

1. Melt the butter in a saucepan, add the onion and fry gently until soft. Add the lamb, celery, tomato purée, ketchup and herbs, with salt and pepper to taste.
2. Divide the mixture into 8 and shape into burgers.
3. Cook the burgers on a barbecue grill for about 15 minutes, turning occasionally.
4. Serve in the split rolls.

Lamb Picnic Stew

Serves: *4*

Preparation time:
10 minutes

Cooking time:
30 minutes

Calories per portion: *255*

450 g (1 lb) neck fillet of **New Zealand Lamb**, *trimmed and cut in small cubes*
1 tbsp plain flour
1 tsp salt
½ tsp ground black pepper
2 tsp ground coriander
1 tbsp oil
1 onion, chopped
1 garlic clove, crushed
2 carrots, sliced
1 orange
439 g (15½ oz) can of butter beans

1. Mix the flour, salt, pepper and coriander in a paper or polythene bag. Put in the lamb cubes and shake until evenly coated.
2. Heat the oil in a saucepan, add the onion, garlic

and carrot and fry, stirring, until browned. Add the meat and fry until browned, stirring frequently to prevent it sticking to the base of the pan.

3. Scrub the orange and pare the zest with a potato peeler. Chop three-quarters of the zest and shred the remainder. Squeeze the juice and add to the pan with the chopped zest. Stir in the butter beans, with the can juices. Bring to the boil, lower the heat and cook for 30 minutes.

4. Rinse a wide-necked vacuum flask with boiling water. Drain thoroughly, then pour in the stew. Rinse out the saucepan with a little boiling water and add to the flask. Seal tightly. The stew will keep hot for about 6 hours. The shredded orange zest may be used as a garnish, if liked. Serve with french bread.

Note: If the stew is to be left in the flask for more than 4 hours, reduce cooking time by 5 minutes.

Lamb Picnic Stew

Granary Cutlet Crisps

Serves: *4*

Preparation time:
5 minutes

Cooking time:
20 minutes

Calories per portion: *760*

8 **New Zealand Lamb** *best end cutlets, skinned and trimmed*

3 tbsp chutney or mint jelly
8 large slices of granary bread
50 g (2 oz) butter, softened

1. Set the oven at 190°C/375°F/Gas Mark 5. Spread the cutlets lightly on both sides with chutney or jelly and place each diagonally across a slice of bread.
2. Overlap the corners of the bread across each cutlet and secure with a wooden cocktail stick.
3. Place the granary cutlets on a baking sheet, spread the top of the bread lightly with butter and bake for about 20 minutes or until the bread is browned. Finish on a barbecue grill, if liked, or serve cold for a picnic spread or packed lunch.

Borek (overleaf)

Travellers' Tales

A recipe can recall precious holiday memories of meals relished in foreign lands. Lamb is loved the world over, so if you experiment with the dishes that follow you could become a gourmet globe-trotter, tucking into tandoori lamb today and tomorrow enjoying a tasty lamb version of the Franco-Russian classic 'Stroganoff'.

Borek

Makes: *30*

Preparation time: *40 minutes*

Cooking time: *40 minutes*

Calories per borek: *60*

450 g (1 lb) minced **New Zealand Lamb**

1 onion, sliced
2 tbsp chopped salted peanuts
25 g (1 oz) sultanas
1 tsp ground cinnamon
salt and pepper
10 sheets of filo pastry
oil for brushing
Garnish:
fresh coriander
lemon wedges

1. Put the lamb into a heavy-bottomed saucepan and heat gently until the fat starts to run. Raise the heat and cook for about 5 minutes until the lamb is well sealed, stirring from time to time.

2. Pour off the excess fat from the pan. Add the onion and cook for 3 minutes, stirring frequently. Stir in the peanuts, sultanas, cinnamon, salt and pepper, then cook for 2 minutes. If the mixture is rather dry, add 2–3 tbsp water.

3. Set the oven at 160°C/325°F/Gas Mark 3. Cut each sheet of filo pastry lengthways into 3 rectangular strips about 8 cm (3 inches) wide. Work quickly, keeping the unused pastry under a dry tea towel, with a dampened tea towel on top. (This will prevent it from drying out and becoming brittle.)

4. Brush a strip of the filo pastry with oil. Place 1

tsp meat mixture about 2.5 cm (1 inch) from the end of the oiled strip. Fold the corner up over the filling to form a triangle, then over the opposite way. Continue folding over the triangle until the strip of pastry is used up.

5. Repeat with the remaining dough strips until all the meat filling has been used. Place the triangles, seam side down, on greased baking sheets, brush lightly with oil and bake for about 30 minutes until crisp and golden.

6. Serve hot or cold as a starter or snack with pre-dinner drinks. Garnish with fresh coriander and lemon wedges. A bowl of plain yogurt makes a good accompaniment.

Moroccan Tagine with Apricots

Serves: *6*

Preparation time:
20 *minutes*

Cooking time:
1¾ *hours*

Calories per portion:
315/350* (see over)

½ leg of **New Zealand Lamb** *(fillet end), about 900 g (2 lb), trimmed and cut into 4 cm (1½-inch) cubes*

3 tbsp oil
1 tsp ground ginger
½ tsp ground cinnamon
1 onion, sliced thinly
300 ml (½ pint) lamb or vegetable stock
450 g (1 lb) fresh apricots or 225 g (8 oz) no-need-to-soak dried apricots
4 tbsp clear honey
2 tbsp chopped fresh parsley
salt and pepper
parsley to garnish

1. Mix half the oil with the ginger and cinnamon in a shallow dish. Add the lamb cubes, turning them in the mixture until well coated.

2. Heat the remaining oil in a flameproof casserole and fry the onion quickly until lightly browned. With a slotted spoon, remove the onion from the pan and set aside.

3. Add the meat to the oil remaining in the casserole and fry gently until lightly browned, taking care not to burn the spices. Add the stock, cover the casserole tightly and simmer for 1 hour, stirring occasionally.

4. Stir the onions into the casserole, cover and continue to cook for 30 minutes more.

5. If using fresh apricots, cut them in half and remove the stones. Add the fresh or dried apricots to the casserole with the honey and parsley. Cover and simmer for 15 minutes more.

6. When the casserole is ready, adjust the seasoning, garnish with parsley and serve. Rice and green salad are the usual accompaniments.

Moroccan Tagine with Apricots

* If dried apricots are used, the higher calorie value applies.

Lamb Stroganoff

Serves: *4*

Preparation time:
10 minutes

Cooking time:
15–20 minutes

Calories per portion: *310*

Lamb Stroganoff

*675 g (1½ lb) boned leg of **New Zealand Lamb**, trimmed and cut into thin strips*

1 tbsp oil
2 onions, sliced thinly
225 g (8 oz) button mushrooms, sliced thinly
2 tbsp tomato purée
2 tbsp sweet sherry
salt and pepper
150 ml (¼ pint) plain yogurt
parsley sprigs and lightly cooked broccoli florets to garnish

1. Heat the oil in a large frying pan, add the onions and mushrooms and fry gently for about 2 minutes or until almost tender.
2. Raise the heat, add the lamb and fry quickly until the meat is evenly browned. Stir in the tomato purée and sherry, with salt and pepper to taste. Bring to the boil, lower the heat and cover. Cook for 10–15 minutes or until the lamb is tender.
3. Just before serving, add the yogurt and stir well. Transfer the stroganoff to a warmed serving dish and garnish with the parsley and broccoli. Serve on a bed of buttered noodles, if liked.

Sosaties

Serves: *4*

Preparation time:
15 minutes + marinating

Cooking time:
10–15 minutes

Calories per portion: *245*

*½ leg of **New Zealand Lamb** (fillet half, approx 500 g/2½ lb), trimmed and cut into thin strips*

2 tsp grated root ginger
2 garlic cloves, crushed
salt and pepper
½ lime, sliced, to garnish
Marinade:
1 tbsp oil
1 onion, chopped
1 tbsp curry powder
1 tbsp sugar
150 ml (¼ pint) water
125 ml (4 fl oz) red wine vinegar
2 bay leaves
1 green chilli, de-seeded and chopped finely, plus extra to garnish

1. Put the lamb into a bowl with the ginger and garlic.
2. Make the marinade. Heat the oil in a small saucepan, add the onion and cook for 3–4 minutes until tender. Stir in the curry powder and sugar and cook for 1 minute. Stir in the remaining ingredients, bring to the boil and cook for 2 minutes. Cool.
3. Pour the marinade over the lamb and mix until the strips are well coated. Cover and marinate in

the refrigerator for at least 2 hours.

4. Drain the lamb, reserving the marinade. Thread the meat on to 4 skewers. Grill for 10–15 minutes, basting occasionally with the reserved marinade. Season with salt and pepper.

5. Garnish the sosaties with lime slices and chopped green chilli. Serve with saffron rice, if liked.

Arni Psito

Serves: 6

Preparation time: *10 minutes*

Cooking time: *2–2½ hours*

Calories per portion: *555*

*1 leg of **New Zealand Lamb**, about 1.8 kg (4 lb), trimmed*

2 garlic cloves, crushed
grated zest and juice of ½ lemon
salt and pepper
25 g (1 oz) butter
2 tbsp oil
125 ml (4 fl oz) lamb or vegetable stock
2 onions, chopped finely
175 g (6 oz) mushrooms, sliced
2 tbsp chopped parsley

1. Set the oven at 230°C/450°F/Gas Mark 8. Combine the garlic and lemon zest in a small bowl. Add 1 tsp salt and a generous amount of freshly ground black pepper. Mix well, then spread the mixture over the surface of the lamb. Place the lamb in a roasting tin.

2. Melt the butter in the oil in a small saucepan. Add the stock and lemon juice, bring to the boil and pour into the roasting tin. Roast the lamb for 15 minutes.

3. Lower the oven temperature to 180°C/350°F/ Gas Mark 4. Mix the onions, mushrooms and parsley and add to the roasting tin. Roast for 1¾–2 hours more.

4. Transfer the lamb to a heated serving dish, surround with the vegetable mixture and serve at once. Rice is the traditional accompaniment.

Oriental Lamb Stir-fry

Serves: *4*

Preparation time:
15 minutes + marinating

Cooking time:
10 minutes

Calories per portion: *240*

450 g (1 lb) **New Zealand Lamb** *neck fillet,
trimmed and cut into thin strips*

2 tbsp soy sauce

2 tsp Chinese five-spice powder

1 tsp ground cumin

1 tbsp oil

100 g (4 oz) mangetout, trimmed

100 g (4 oz) baby sweetcorn, halved

6 spring onions, trimmed and chopped

100 g (4 oz) button mushrooms, quartered

100 g (4 oz) broccoli florets

250 g (8 oz) beansprouts

salt and pepper

Oriental Lamb Stir-fry

1. Combine the first five ingredients in a bowl.
Mix well, cover and marinate for at least 2 hours.

2. Heat a wok or large frying-pan. Add the lamb and marinade and cook, stirring constantly, until the meat is sealed.

3. Stir in the mangetout, sweetcorn, spring onions, mushrooms and broccoli. Fry quickly, stirring constantly, until the vegetables are just starting to soften. Stir in the beansprouts.

4. As soon as the beansprouts are heated through, tip the contents of the wok or frying-pan into a heated serving dish, add salt and pepper to taste and serve at once.

Lamb and Peach Pilaff

Serves: *6*

Preparation time:
20 minutes + soaking

Cooking time:
1¼ hours

Calories per portion: *330*

*½ shoulder of **New Zealand Lamb** (blade half), about 900 g (2 lb), boned, trimmed and cut into 2.5 cm (1-inch) cubes*
25 g (1 oz) butter
2 onions, sliced
½ tsp ground cinnamon
4 cardamoms
1 bay leaf
1 tsp ground cumin
100 g (4 oz) dried peaches, soaked overnight
2 tbsp lemon juice
1 red pepper, cored, de-seeded and sliced
225 g (8 oz) long-grain rice
salt
2 tbsp chopped parsley, to garnish

1. Heat the butter in a large frying-pan, add the onions and fry for about 5 minutes or until soft.

2. Add the lamb to the pan and stir until evenly browned. Stir in the cinnamon, cardamoms, bay leaf and cumin.

3. Drain the peaches, chop them roughly and stir them into the lamb mixture with the lemon juice. Add water to cover, then bring to the boil. Lower the heat, cover the pan and simmer for 30 minutes.

4. Add the sliced red pepper, replace the lid and simmer for 30 minutes more.

5. Meanwhile cook the rice in boiling salted water for about 12 minutes or until tender. Drain well. Stir carefully into the lamb mixture and heat through gently for 10 minutes. Remove the bay leaf.
6. Sprinkle with parsley and serve at once.

Tandoori Lamb

Serves: *4*

Preparation time:
20 minutes + marinating

Cooking time:
1–1¼ hours

Calories per portion: *170*

*½ leg of **New Zealand Lamb** (fillet end), about 800 g (1¾ lb), trimmed and cubed*

1 onion, quartered
2 garlic cloves, crushed
thinly pared zest of ½ lemon
6 tbsp plain yogurt
3 tbsp wine vinegar
salt and pepper
½ tsp paprika
¼ tsp chilli powder
½ tsp ground fenugreek
1 tsp ground ginger
Garnish:
lettuce leaves
raw onion rings
lemon wedges

1. Chop the onion, garlic and lemon zest finely by hand or in a blender or food processor. Add the yogurt, vinegar, salt, pepper and spices. Blend until smooth or stir in thoroughly by hand.
2. Put the lamb cubes in a shallow dish large enough to take them in a single layer. Pour over the yogurt mixture and mix until well coated. Cover the dish and marinate for at least 6 hours and up to 24 hours in a cool place. Turn the meat over in the marinade several times.
3. Set the oven at 180°C/350°F/Gas Mark 4. Transfer the lamb cubes and marinade to a casserole and bake for 1–1¼ hours or until tender.
4. Serve on a bed of lettuce leaves, garnished with onion rings and lemon wedges.

Tomato Bredie

Serves: *4*

Preparation time:
20 minutes

Cooking time:
2½–3 hours

Calories per portion: *750*

900 g (2 lb) **New Zealand stewing lamb**
2 tbsp plain flour
salt and pepper
1 tbsp oil
2 onions, sliced
6 large ripe tomatoes, skinned and chopped
1 small red chilli, de-seeded and chopped
1 tbsp sugar

Note: Wear gloves when chopping chillies or wash your hands very thoroughly afterwards. Carelessly rubbing eyes with fingers that have been in contact with chillies can cause severe irritation.

1. Mix the flour, salt and pepper in a paper or polythene bag, add the lamb and toss lightly to coat.
2. Heat the oil in a large heavy-bottomed saucepan, add the onions and fry gently for 2 minutes. Add the meat and fry until well browned.
3. Add the tomatoes, chilli and sugar, with salt and pepper to taste. It should not be necessary to add any additional liquid.
4. Bring the mixture to the boil, lower the heat, cover tightly and simmer for 2–3 hours until the sauce is thick and the meat is very tender. Check the bredie frequently and add a little water if necessary.
5. Skim off any fat from the surface of the bredie. Serve at once, with brown rice, if liked.

Salonika Steaks

Serves: *4*

Preparation time:
10–15 minutes

Cooking time:
30 minutes

Calories per portion: *420*

4 **New Zealand Lamb** *leg steaks or chump chops, trimmed*
salt and pepper
2 tbsp oil
2 garlic cloves, crushed
2 onions, sliced
397 g (14 oz) can of chopped tomatoes
1 tbsp tomato purée
1 tsp dried oregano or marjoram
150 ml (¼ pint) lamb or vegetable stock
1 aubergine, trimmed and chopped
150 ml (¼ pint) plain yogurt
1 egg, beaten

1. Season the lamb lightly with salt and pepper. Heat the oil in a large frying-pan, add the steaks and quickly brown them on both sides. Using tongs or a slotted spoon, remove the lamb from the pan.

2. Add the garlic and onions to the oil remaining in the pan and fry gently until soft. Drain off any excess fat. Add the tomatoes, tomato purée, herbs and stock, with salt and pepper to taste. Bring to the boil, then lower the heat and add the aubergine.

3. Replace the lamb in the sauce. Simmer for 15–20 minutes, until the meat is tender and the sauce is thick and pulpy. Adjust the seasoning.

4. Heat the grill to its maximum setting. Beat the yogurt and egg together in a bowl. Spoon over the top of the chops. Immediately place the pan under the grill and cook until the custard topping is lightly browned and set. Serve at once.

Salonika Steaks

Microwave Magic

A microwave can be a considerable asset when it comes to cooking New Zealand Lamb. It can't perform miracles – it won't turn scrag end into a succulent stew in the time it takes you to prepare the accompanying vegetables – but it does produce wonderful results with tender cuts like cutlets, neck fillet and chump chops and it is also perfect for cooking mince dishes.

All the recipes in this section have been tested on 700-watt microwave ovens. Adjust the timings if the power output on your oven is different. If using a 650-watt appliance, allow 15 seconds more per minute; if using a 500-watt appliance, allow 40 seconds more per minute. Check food frequently and follow instructions for turning, stirring or rearranging.

Lamb in the microwave

Here are a few simple tips for successful microwave results every time:

● Lamburgers, noisettes, meatballs and steaks should be evenly spaced around the rim of a microwave-proof plate or round dish, where they will receive equal amounts of microwave energy.

● Irregularly shaped foods, like chops or cutlets, should be arranged with the thinner ends to the centre, where they will receive less energy.

● Follow instructions in individual recipes for using small pieces of foil to shield areas likely to overcook. Always check your own manufacturer's handbook first – and never allow foil to touch the sides of the microwave cabinet.

● Always check that the dish or bowl selected is not only suitable for use in a microwave, but will fit in your appliance. Many a cook has prepared a lasagne or moussaka only to find the turntable will not rotate with the dish in the oven!

● Chops and smaller cuts will look and taste better if seared in a frying-pan or on a browning dish. Heat the browning dish according to the manufacturer's instructions.

● Small roasts must be thawed thoroughly (see page 00). Roast at Medium High for 11 minutes per 450 g (1 lb). Put the joint on a rack in a shallow dish to ensure the meat does not 'stew' in its own juices. Turn the joint halfway through cooking. When cooked, cover with foil and let stand for 15 minutes.

Koftas

Serves: *4*

Preparation time:
10 minutes

Cooking time:
6 minutes + 3 minutes standing

Setting: *Full Power*

Calories per portion: *310*

450 g (1 lb) minced **New Zealand Lamb**
2 onions, grated
50 g (2 oz) soft white breadcrumbs
1 egg yolk
2-3 tbsp chopped fresh parsley
1 tbsp lemon juice
salt and pepper
flour for shaping
lemon wedges to garnish

1. Mix the lamb, onions, breadcrumbs, egg yolk, parsley and lemon juice in a bowl, with salt and pepper to taste.
2. Divide the mixture into 4 portions. With lightly floured hands, form 1 portion of the mixture into a sausage shape around a wooden kebab skewer. Shape the remaining koftas in the same way.
3. Place the koftas on a plate and cook on Full Power for 6 minutes, turning and rearranging once. Cover and leave to stand for 3 minutes.
4. Garnish with lemon wedges. Serve on a bed of brown rice or in hollowed pitta breads, with lettuce, cucumber and onion rings, if liked.

Sweet and Sour Lamb Kebabs

Serves: *6*

Preparation time:
15 minutes + marinating

Cooking time:
3 minutes + preheating browning dish + 5 minutes standing

Setting: *Full Power*

Calories per portion: *275*

900 g (2 lb) lean **New Zealand Lamb** *fillet, trimmed and cut into 5 cm (2-inch) cubes*
4 tbsp pineapple juice
2 tbsp clear honey
2 tbsp light soy sauce
1 tbsp tomato purée
1 tsp cornflour
salt and pepper
12 cherry tomatoes
2 red onions, cut into wedges
2 tbsp oil
bay leaves to garnish

1. Place the lamb in a shallow dish large enough to take all the cubes in a single layer.

2. Mix the pineapple juice, honey, soy sauce, tomato purée, cornflour, salt and pepper in a jug, pour over the lamb and turn to coat. Cover and marinate for at least 2 hours.

3. Drain the lamb, reserving the marinade. Thread the meat on to 6 bamboo skewers, alternating with the cherry tomatoes and onions.

4. Pour the oil on to a microwave browning dish. Preheat the dish according to the manufacturer's instructions. Place the kebabs on top and cook on Full Power for 1½ minutes.

5. Turn the kebabs over, baste with the reserved marinade and cook on Full Power for 1½ minutes, basting once with the marinade. Remove from the microwave oven and allow to stand for 5 minutes.

6. Garnish the kebabs with the bay leaves. Serve with rice, if liked.

Spicy Potato and Lamb Bake

Serves: *4*

Preparation time:
15 minutes

Cooking time:
17 minutes + preheating browning dish

Setting: *Full Power*

Calories per portion: *365*

---

*4 **New Zealand Lamb** chump chops*
2 tbsp oil
2.5 cm (1-inch) piece of root ginger, cut into sticks
1 onion, sliced
1 tbsp ground coriander
1 tsp cumin seeds
3 medium-size potatoes, cut into bite-size pieces and par-boiled
4 tbsp lamb stock
salt and freshly ground black pepper
snipped chives to garnish

1. Cut the chops in half. Pour the oil into a bowl, add the ginger and cook on Full Power for 1 minute. Add the onion, cover and cook on Full Power for for 4 minutes.

2. Stir in the coriander and cumin seeds and cook on Full Power for 1 minute.

3. Add the potatoes. Pour over the stock, salt and pepper. Cook on Full Power for 5 minutes, stirring once, until tender. Remove from oven.

4. Preheat a browning dish according to the manufacturer's instructions. Add the chops and cook on Full Power for 2 minutes. Turn over and cook on Full Power for 2 minutes.

5. Add the lamb to the potato mixture and cook on Full Power for 2 minutes. Garnish with the chives.

6. Serve immediately with naan bread and dips.

Spicy Potato and Lamb Bake

Lamb Paprikash

Serves: *3*

Preparation time:
10 minutes + preheating browning dish

Cooking time:
16 minutes

Setting: *Full Power*

Calories per portion: *540*

Lamb Paprikash

*900 g (2 lb) shoulder of **New Zealand Lamb**, boned and cut into 2.5 cm (1-inch) cubes*

2 tbsp oil
1 onion, chopped
1 garlic clove, crushed
1 tbsp paprika
150 ml (¼ pint) lamb stock
150 ml (¼ pint) soured cream
salt and pepper
a sprig of coriander to garnish

1. Pour 1 tbsp of oil over a browning dish and preheat according to manufacturer's instructions. Add the lamb and cook on Full Power for 2 minutes. Stir and cook for a further 1 minute. Remove from oven.

2. Pour the remaining oil into a large bowl. Add the onion and garlic, cover, and cook on Full Power for 4 minutes, stirring twice, until softened.

3. Add the paprika and cook on Full Power for 1 minute. Stir in the lamb and stock. Cover with microwave and pierce it. Cook on Full Power for 8 minutes, until the lamb is tender. Remove from the oven.

4. Stir in the soured cream and season to taste. Garnish with the coriander sprig.

Lamb Cutlets with Orange and Redcurrant Sauce

Serves: *4*

Preparation time: *16 minutes*

Cooking time: *preheating browning dish + 5½ minutes + 1 minute standing*

Setting: *Full Power*

Calories per portion: *490*

8 ***New Zealand Lamb*** *cutlets*
1 tbsp oil
227 g (8 oz) jar of redcurrant jelly
2 tbsp red wine
2 tbsp tomato purée
pared zest of 1 orange, cut into small strips
salt and pepper
Garnish:
orange zest strips
lime zest strips

1. Pour the oil over a microwave browning dish. Preheat the dish according to the manufacturer's instructions. Arrange the lamb cutlets on the dish, with the thin ends towards the centre. Cook on Full Power for 4 minutes, turning the cutlets over and rearranging them after 2 minutes. Remove from the oven and allow to stand for 5 minutes.

2. Meanwhile mix the redcurrant jelly, wine and tomato purée in a bowl. Add the orange zest strips, with salt and pepper to taste. Cook on Full Power for 1½ minutes, stirring occasionally. Allow to stand for 1 minute.

3. Transfer the lamb to a serving dish and pour the sauce over. Garnish with the strips of orange and lime zest and serve at once, with mangetout, if liked.

Creamy Lamb Pinwheels

Serves: *4*

Preparation time: *20 minutes*

Cooking time: *preheating browning dish + 7½ minutes + 5 minutes standing*

Setting: *Full Power*

Calories per portion: *695*

900 g (2 lb) boned best end of **New Zealand Lamb**, *trimmed*
2 tbsp oil
1 onion, chopped
1 garlic clove, crushed
78 g (2¾ oz) packet of garlic and herb soft cheese
1 tbsp chopped mint
salt and pepper
25 g (1 oz) soft white breadcrumbs
1 egg yolk
185 g (6½ oz) jar of mint jelly
4 tbsp boiling lamb or chicken stock
mint sprigs to garnish

1. Pour 1 tbsp of the oil into a large bowl. Add the onion and garlic, cover and cook on Full Power for 3½ minutes, stirring twice, until soft. Remove from the oven and cool.
2. Lay the lamb flat on a work surface. Stir the cheese, chopped mint, salt, pepper, breadcrumbs and egg yolk into the onions. Spread evenly over the meat, carefully roll up and secure with string.
3. Slice the lamb roll into 5 cm (2-inch) pinwheels. Pour the remaining oil over a browning dish. Preheat the dish according to the manufacturer's instructions. Add the lamb and cook on Full Power for 1½ minutes. Turn over and cook on Full Power for 1 minute, then remove from the oven and cover with microwave cling film. Allow to stand for 5 minutes.
4. Melt the mint jelly in the stock in a large bowl on Full Power for 1½ minutes. Arrange the lamb pinwheels on serving plates, spoon sauce over each and garnish with mint. Serve with courgette and celery sticks, if liked.

Minced Lamb Pasta

Serves: *4*	
Preparation time: *10 minutes*	
Cooking time: *16 minutes + 10 minutes standing*	
Setting: *Full Power*	
Calories per portion: *842*	

450 g (1 lb) minced **New Zealand Lamb**
2 tbsp oil
225 g (8 oz) smoked streaky bacon
1 onion, chopped
1 garlic clove, crushed
2 celery sticks, sliced
1 tbsp plain flour
150 ml (¼ pint) lamb stock
2 tbsp tomato purée
1 tbsp quince jelly or redcurrant jelly
2 tsp dried mixed herbs
salt and pepper
225 g (8 oz) pasta shells, cooked
225 g (8 oz) Cotswold cheese with herbs
grated parmesan cheese to garnish

Minced Lamb Pasta

1. Place the oil, lamb and bacon in a large bowl. Cook on Full Power for 7 minutes, stirring occasionally. Stir in the onion, garlic and celery and cook on Full Power for 1 minute.

2. Add the stock, tomato purée, quince or redcurrant jelly, mixed herbs, salt and pepper. Cover and cook on Full Power for 4 minutes, stirring occasionally. Remove from the heat and stir in the pasta. Cover and allow to stand for 10 minutes.

3. Spoon on to warmed serving plates. Cut the cheese into thin strips and create a lattice design on top. Cook one at a time on Full Power for 1 minute, until the cheese is melted.

4. Serve immediately, sprinkled with parmesan.

Chump Chops with Apricot Sauce

Serves: *4*

Preparation time: *10 minutes*

Cooking time: *10 minutes*

Setting: *Full Power*

Calories per portion: *270*

*4 **New Zealand Lamb** chump chops, 2.5 cm (1 inch) thick, trimmed*

215 g (7½ oz) can of apricots in natural juice

1 tsp arrowroot

1 tsp Meaux mustard

1 tbsp lemon juice

1–2 tbsp clear honey

a few sprigs of rosemary to garnish

1. Arrange the chops in a ring around the rim of a plate. Cover and cook on Full Power for 6 minutes, turning over once.

2. Drain the apricots, reserving the juice. Blend the arrowroot with 2 tbsp of the apricot juice in a jug. Stir in the mustard, lemon juice, honey and remaining apricot juice.

3. Transfer the cooked chops to a heated serving dish. Cook the apricot sauce on Full Power for 2½ minutes, stirring frequently. Meanwhile chop the apricots.

4. Add the apricots to the thickened sauce and cook for 30 seconds more on Full Power to warm through. Spoon the sauce over the chops and reheat on Full Power for 45 seconds.

5. Garnish with rosemary and serve at once.

Moussaka

Serves: *6*

Preparation time:
25 minutes

Cooking time:
30 minutes + 2 minutes standing

Setting: *Full Power*

Calories per portion: *565*

900 g (2 lb) minced **New Zealand Lamb**
2 aubergines, cut in 5 mm (¼-inch) slices
salt and pepper
25 g (1 oz) butter
225 g (8 oz) onions, chopped finely
2 garlic cloves, crushed
4 tbsp tomato purée
1 tsp dried oregano
a pinch of ground nutmeg
1 tbsp chopped parsley
40 g (1½ oz) plain flour
150 ml (¼ pint) lamb or vegetable stock
Sauce:
25 g (1 oz) butter, cut in pieces
25 g (1 oz) plain flour
300 ml (½ pint) milk
75 g (3 oz) Cheddar cheese, grated
1 egg, beaten
To finish:
1 tbsp chopped parsley
grated nutmeg

1. Put the aubergine slices in a colander, sprinkle generously with salt and leave for 20 minutes to draw out the liquid.

2. Rinse the aubergines, drain thoroughly and place in a deep dish. Cover and cook on Full Power for 4 minutes. Set aside.

3. Put the butter in a large bowl with the onions and garlic. Cook on Full Power for 4–5 minutes until soft and transparent. Add the lamb, tomato purée, oregano, nutmeg, parsley and flour, with salt and pepper to taste. Mix well. Gradually stir in the stock. Cover and cook on Full Power for 14 minutes, stirring every 3–4 minutes.

4. Meanwhile make the sauce. Combine the butter, flour and milk in a large measuring jug or bowl. Whisk until well mixed.

5. Remove the lamb mixture from the oven and

leave to stand. Cook the sauce on Full Power for 30 seconds. Whisk, then cook for 3 minutes more, whisking frequently. The sauce should be smooth and thick. Add the cheese and egg, whisking constantly.

6. Layer the aubergine and lamb mixture in a large dish, finishing with a layer of aubergine. Pour the sauce over the top and cook on Full Power for 4 minutes more. Stand for 2 minutes.

7. Sprinkle with grated nutmeg, garnish with parsley and serve at once.

Notes for American and Australian readers

Although a teaspoon measure holds about 5 ml wherever it is used, there is no universal tablespoon measure. British and American measures do not differ widely (a British tablespoon holds 17.7 ml, the American 14.2 ml). For convenience sake both British and American tablespoons are regarded as being equivalent to 15 ml, but the Australian tablespoon is larger, with a capacity of 20 ml. Readers using Australian measures should therefore make some minor adjustments.

British/American	Australian
1 tsp	1 tsp
l tbsp	1 tbsp
2/3 tbsp	2 tbsp
3½/4 tbsp	3 tbsp
4/5 tbsp	3½ tbsp

The Imperial pint (in use in Britain and Australia) equals 20 fl oz, whereas the American pint is 16 fl oz. Americans use the 8 oz cup measure for both solids and liquids. The following comparisons may be helpful:

Imperial	American
450 g (1 lb) butter or margarine	2 cups
450 g (1 lb) flour	4 cups

100 g (4 oz) cheese, grated	1 cup
50 g (2 oz) soft white breadcrumbs	1 cup
200 g (7 oz) long-grain white rice	1 cup
225 g (8 oz) brown rice	1 cup
450 g (1 lb) kidney beans	1½ cups
100 g (4 oz) sliced mushrooms	l cup
¼ pint liquid	⅔ cup
½ pint liquid	1¼ cups
¾ pint liquid	2 cups
1 pint liquid	2½ cups

American terms or substitutes for items used in this book are listed below.

British	American
aubergine	eggplant
cling film	plastic wrap
cornflour	cornstarch
courgette	zucchini
cream (single)	cream (light)
cream (double)	cream (heavy)
flour (plain)	flour (all-purpose)
frying-pan	skillet
lard	shortening
mangetout	snow peas
spring onion	scallion
stock cubes	bouillon cubes
tomato purée	tomato paste